MISUNDERSTOOD MONEY

MISUNDERSTOOD MONEY

Stop Voting Away Your Money

Jay Hingst

Copyright © Jay Hingst.

All rights reserved. No part of this book may be reproduced in any form or by any electronic or mechanical means, including information storage and retrieval systems, without permission in writing from the publisher, except by reviewers, who may quote brief passages in a review.

ISBN: 978-1-63649-968-0   (Paperback Edition)
ISBN: 978-1-63649-969-7   (Hardcover Edition)
ISBN: 978-1-63649-967-3   (E-book Edition)

Book Ordering Information

Phone Number: 347-901-4929 or 347-901-4920
Email: info@globalsummithouse.com
Global Summit House
www.globalsummithouse.com

Printed in the United States of America

CONTENTS

Preface vii

Introduction to money 1
    Barter Trade And The Exchange Rate 2
    Precious Metals – Value And Demand 4
    Receipts 5
    Receipts And Exchange Rates 6
    Paper Money 6

Inflation and the pay rate 8

Money, Taxation and tax systems 11
    Money 13
    Government And Money 14
    Impact Of Taxes 14
    Hierarchical Tax Accumulation 15
    Imaginary Taxes 16
    Do The Math! 17

The fallacy of wage increases and savings 19
    Minimum Wage Raises 19

Paying people what they need 25
    Buying Support With Your Money 26

Money: How about introducing a new standard of measure? 29
    Interstate Exchange Rate 30
    Legal Theft 32
    Pills Taxes And Liability 33

Rich people and money 35
    Let The Other Guy Pay For It 39

Governments: Production and Allocative Efficiency 44
    Road Taxes For Electric Vehicles 47
    The Government Should Do More..48
    They Haven't Done It Right..50
    Side Note 51

Teaching about Money – Beyond the numbers 53
    The Death Of Brick And Mortar...56

Taxation – The Laffer Curve and Government Deception........... 60

Tax payers and tax collectors 67

Printing money...74

PREFACE

This book is inspired by my recent observation of how many people don't understand money and how it works or what it does.

Our schools are failing society in this aspect. Years ago, many children grew up working in family businesses, be it farm or store or another form of endeavor. These children worked with their families and learned many things that the schools have never taken the responsibility to educate them on.

They learned that if you did not plant, you would not have grain for later. If you did not feed the livestock, you did not have meat, eggs, milk, etc. They learned at an early age that doing things or not doing things had consequences. They also learned that those consequences might be immediate or long term, but ultimately, they discovered these lessons directly.

Over time, some of these jobs that the children did became more dangerous, and governments took notice and passed rules that limited what tasks children were allowed to perform. While this meant to protect the children, it limited the number of roles that the children could play and learn out of. While the government was trying to protect the children, they made no effort to replace the lost education when children were directly involved in production or creation.

Our education has never picked up the slack. This education only teaches one plus one equals two, and two plus two equals four. It shows that two apples plus two apples equal four apples. What is missing is the relative value of each of the items. Two apples plus two apples do not equal four apples if one of those apples is rotten. There is nothing said about the value of the items added. A child working on a farm would have experienced this first hand. He would not necessarily have been taught this. Instead, he would have learned it through experience. Experience has always been a great teacher.

As I say, the education of our children has been lacking, be it in a government-run school, private school, religious school, or another educational endeavor; none of them put "value" into their equations. They may be very good at teaching the basics, as the board of education defines it, but they do not teach the basics of value. These basics would include the natural laws that are involved. These are the things that children working with their parents would have been exposed to naturally.

This reason, I have written this book – to try to put the value into money. Everyone seems to think that money is valuable. It is not; the things that are bought and sold using money are, but money has no value. It is just an instantaneous means of exchange. A given amount of money may be exchanged for something today, but next week, it may take a different amount of money to make the same exchange.

INTRODUCTION TO MONEY

Money is an essential element of our lives, yet our societies misunderstand the usage of money to great heights! Everyone uses it, yet they do not know how it works or what it is. Money has no intrinsic value; it does not exist except in the acceptance of its use by the people who use it.

That being said, many people try to manipulate it. They think just making more "dollars" means that you have more money (VALUE), but I beg to differ. We will come back to this later on; for now, we get into a brief history lesson about the origins of money.

The history of money has no real traceable origins because, honestly, we hear of silver and gold being used as the money back in the Biblical days of Abraham thousands of years ago. However, coming closer to us, we hear of means of trade such as 'barter trade,' where people could exchange different goods for another. For example, the ones with a lot of flour could exchange it for costumes, as an example. This also depended on many facts, like, the person being given the flour must be satisfied that the amount they are getting is the fair value of the garments they are giving off.

As this practice went on, it became apparent that some families had more of one thing than the other, resulting in absolute advantage when compared against each other's ability to trade, buy, and store goods. Families with wealth became powerful over time.

Nevertheless, we learn that, about 600BC, the first real coins were minted by Lydia's King Alyattes. This first official currency was made of electrum, which is a natural mix of silver and gold. These coins helped to enhance trade between nations during the time, thus creating wealth that separated these same countries. Fast forward to today, we still live among the same conditions of 'silver and gold' now in the form of banknotes and coins.

Now that we have these, people began to measure wealth in monetary terms. But, the real value is never in the number of dollars you have in your account, but it is the value you have, including your physical wealth. My son gave me a defunct banknote from Zimbabwe, which was a 10,000,000,000 dollar note. Yes, that is ten billion (with a "B") dollars, yet at the time, it was not worth a lot as they were printing trillion-dollar notes over there. But the worth of their dollar was still a dollar – in that country. This is a classic example of how the number of dollars you might have in the account might not mean you're wealthy.

It is not the number of dollars (or pieces of paper) that is important when counting wealth; but, it is the exchange rate "VALUE" of the currency that counts. For example, a billion-dollar note in Zimbabwe during that time could buy you a single US dollar, and, whereas someone could buy a whole small town with 10 billion US dollars, in Zimbabwe, that could only buy a loaf of bread.

BARTER TRADE AND THE EXCHANGE RATE

Speaking of how much the Zimbabwean Dollar could buy of the US Dollar brought us to this sub-heading – the Exchange Rate. This can be explained in two forms, for the sake of this book – first, regarding barter trade, secondly, in terms of our current monetary terms. With barter trade or bartering, the exchange rate was the agreed-upon quantity of one item for another during a trade or an exchange. The exchange rate was based on the availability of one item, as compared to another. That is, if there was a bumper harvest of apples and they were readily available, and there was a less than stellar crop of wheat, the exchange rate would be more than a bushel of apples for a bushel of wheat.

I learned a bit about the exchange rate when I was 10-12 years old. My folks would occasionally go over to the bar across the street from our hardware store and have a drink. I would sometimes go over with them and have a coke. We were there one time, and a patron asked the bartender how much the cigars were. The bartender replied, 25 cents apiece, 3 for a dollar. To which the patron replied, I'll take 3. The dollar was still worth a dollar, but what was its value, three cigars, or four? This is why I say a dollar has no intrinsic value. Just chasing the dollar does not bring extra value to your worth.

We have been seeing this over the years, especially considering inflation and wage increases. When wages go up, the "value" of the dollar goes down! We will explore more on this in the following chapter.

Nevertheless, we explore more factors that determine the exchange rate in the barter system of trade. Below are some of the factors to consider;

- Does the seller need or want the items being offered for his product?

- Does the farmer want more apples?

- He may want more bushels of apples for his wheat, or he may not even want the deal at all.

If the seller does not want the deal but would like something else in exchange, the buyer may opt to see if he can exchange his apples with someone else to get the desired item. He then can use that to obtain the wheat he wanted. But, if the buyer keeps on struggling to get takers for his deal, his apples, in his eyes, could be reduced in value because 'they are not getting him what he wants.'

Therefore, we reiterate this fact – that money is measured by what it can get you, not by the amount you have in your account.

However, as the buyer seeks more takers of his apples in exchange for wheat, it could lead to a lot of trading with many other people to get what the buyer wants. This would be very inefficient and time-consuming.

PRECIOUS METALS – VALUE AND DEMAND

Money is determined by its value, which in itself, is determined by the level of demand and supply.

Precious metals and gems were highly sought after for their decorative values, thus giving them intrinsic value. These items became not only a sought-after item in themselves, but they also became a common item to use for barter in place of things that people may not have wanted or needed.

Silver is a good example. For many years, there was a lot of silver required to make films, and it resulted in a rise in its price. As the need has diminished, due to the electronic capture of images not needing film anymore, the demand for silver has dropped. As the market declined, the "value" of silver has also dropped, and it is no longer the most talked about commodity right now.

Precious metals and jewels, unlike other commodities like wheat and maize, had preservative value in that they did not rot or go bad, and could be used, or sold, at a much later date when the price had improved. This freed the person from having to make immediate trades for things that they would not be in urgent need.

Also, using these items had the added benefit of a more fixed exchange rate, they did not have the rapid swings that occurred because of crop conditions acting on the exchange rate and the like. This does not mean that the exchange rate would always be the same. It could vary due to economic conditions such as drought caused shortages or overproduction.

A gold ring, for example, might trade for a bushel of wheat now. Years from now, the same gold ring would still sell for a bushel of wheat grain. Its intrinsic value would stay the same, meaning the exchange rate would be relatively constant.

Recently, I heard that 100 miles down in the crust of the Earth, there is a large layer of Diamonds. If this layer were to be mined, the value of the diamonds would plummet and become virtually worthless, explaining the law of supply and demand. Excessive supply reduces the value of the item.

There is also an asteroid in the solar system that has many millions of tons of gold. Again, if that were to be mined, the value of gold would plummet and not be worth any more than iron. The gold would not have any real value, and its resulting value would be that of the cost of obtaining and processing the metal.

RECEIPTS

As organized trading developed, that is, middlemen that had many different items available to trade, another way of holding barter value for future use came into being in the form of a "receipt". This receipt was some form of document that the seller gets for his items that can be used or accumulated for a later date in trade for some other item.

I recently heard (on the TV show "Curse of Oak Island") that the Knights Templar used a form of receipts to take deposits in one area and would repay them in another area so that travelers would not be carrying large amounts of precious metals or jewels. This prevented theft by highwaymen. One thing, they would keep the deposits if something happened to the person and they were unable to claim their property.

RECEIPTS AND EXCHANGE RATES

Receipts have no intrinsic value and are subject to the creator's economic condition. If the creator should go broke, the receipt becomes worthless. Also, it is subject to exchange rate fluctuation. If the value of the receipted item goes up, you can buy more, and if it goes down, you can buy less. This is also subject to the receipt creator's whim.

PAPER MONEY

Paper money grew out of the gold and silver mining. The miners would take their findings to an assay office where they would exchange it for a receipt. These receipts were based on the number of ounces of the bullion traded. Now, these receipts were subject to the same problems as the other receipts.

They started being issued by large bullion houses that were very stable. The miners could take these receipts to the general store, and elsewhere, to buy their needs. As these receipts became more widely accepted, they became a de facto currency.

The government and the politicians became acutely aware of these receipts. And, one of the problems with them was the wide number of different entities issuing them. The government started issuing banknotes that were based on the value of gold. The government used actual bullion to back those notes.

For a long time, our paper currency was based on gold or silver through what was known as gold or silver certificates. It was a promissory note to exchange the note for a given amount of gold or silver – but could also be used as a medium of exchange for something else. The problem was that inflation in the use of the paper money caused these certificates to be worth less than their amount of promised precious metal at a later date. And, to combat this problem, the politicians and the government decided to drop the tie between the paper money and the underlying metal. They took us off of the "gold standard".

With this, the value of the "dollar" was allowed to float as it was not tied to anything, meaning that the dollar had no intrinsic value. More savvy people saw an opportunity to manipulate the value of the dollar after it was untied to the gold standard. It also gave the less savvy the ability to unknowingly manipulate the value of the dollar to their own loss. One way was to have an arbitrary wage raise, which reduced the value of saved dollars. The dollar's value is the value of the economy divided by the number of dollars in circulation. That is to say, the more dollars printed the less value the dollar has (Inflation).

INFLATION AND THE PAY RATE

Inflation measures the general increase in price levels. It is measured using a basket of selected essential goods that people consume in their homes. This basket's prices are tracked, and their month to month move (using the Consumer Price Index) determines the level of inflation in any country. More so, inflation is also caused by taxes. Taxes become part of doing business and are added into the cost of the goods or services.

For the sake of this chapter, it is essential to understand that these basic items' prices are always on the rise, sometimes slower, and sometimes at a higher pace, depending on each country. As the prices are rising, wages, sometimes rise at a slower rate, or they don't rise at all. These essential goods we are speaking of include the likes of bread and cooking oil that is used daily in people's homes.

However, for prices to increase, many factors come into play; for example, the level of money supply in the economy. Inflation is the result of arbitrary pay increases, which results in more money supply in circulation. One of the biggest drivers of these pay increases is the idea that people should be paid according to their needs instead of their production value.

But, the one thing that a worker offers are his hours of work. These are the same, whether he is being paid one dollar per hour or one thousand dollars per hour. That being said, the only reason for someone making more than someone else must be the amount of value produced per hour of work.

To give context to the above, a coal miner loading one ton of coal is only worth half as much as a coal miner loading two tons of coal in the same amount of time. If a decision is made that the slower worker gets paid the same amount as the faster one, this will cause inflation. The reason for it being inflationary is that the price of a ton of coal will have to go up to cover the extra cost of loading it. This increase in loading costs has a direct impact on the price of coal, and thus, inflation. Why is this move ending up causing inflation? Well, coal is used to produce many things; one of them is electricity. If the cost of its production rises, coal producers will push the cost to consumers of the coal (local governments or electricity producers), who, in turn, push the costs down to their own consumers. These include producers of different goods and services. These will also respond by raising the price of their products to cover for increased costs of acquiring electricity. This is how inflation is caused, among many other reasons.

Nevertheless, while the slower worker may see an increase in his pay, he will also see an increase in the cost of things he buys in the future. Also, he will see an increase in his taxes, as one of the dirty little secrets of inflation that is used to replace the value lost in monetary assets and liabilities of the government.

When I was growing up, my extended family had a grocery store and a hardware store. I worked in both stocking shelves and helping customers with various needs of theirs. My extended family eventually sold the grocery store, but back then, there were no computers to help track inventory. One thing that my father told me that finally caused the closing of the hardware store was inflation.

This store was in a rural area, and the level of business was moderate over there. Things would stay on the shelves for quite some time before they were sold off. A good example of this was the hammers, as my father pointed out. They would buy six hammers, put a normal mark-up on them, and put them on the shelf for customers to see, and possibly buy them. Even as they displayed them like that, it would take many months or years to sell the six hammers. As my dad said, when the last one sold, and they went to order more hammers, what they would have to pay for the new ones was equal to, or more than the last one they sold. It resulted in instant losses for the shop.

This means that due to inflation, to replace items on the shelves would cost more than they sold the last ones for. And it resulted in losses that occurred over and over again. As restocking was being done, they would find themselves dipping into their savings to replenish the stock instead of using profits from the last consignment. This condemned them to even having to dig deeper for daily survival. Something that was depressing, especially given that they were running a business.

So, without all the computers, etc., to help track the cost changes caused by inflation and people just getting paid more money, the value of inventory would end up being unable to cover for the costs of continually running the business. Large businesses could afford extra staff just to track these cost changes and revalue their stock, but a small business did not have the resources.

How then does this kill small businesses? They are killed because of what I call inventory taxes. How? The taxes on utilities, and all the cost that keeps the lights on the inventory do the damage. Many of these taxes and costs accrue daily, therefore, adding to the cost of having the goods sit on the shelves. So, unless the items sell frequently, these taxes raise the cost of these goods to a point where there is no profit left for the merchant! Other sellers that have a higher turn-over of these items can sell them for less. If these merchants can not compete, they go out of business.

MONEY, TAXATION AND TAX SYSTEMS

"There is no worse tyranny than to force a man to pay for what he does not want merely because you think it would be good for him."

— Robert A. Heinlein; *The Moon is a Harsh Mistress*

The tax system was not meant to be a support to the people. Taxes were needed to fund the functions of the government and to provide major infrastructure items such as the postal system and roads. These infrastructure items were to promote trade not to be a direct help to any people or groups. It is only in the politicians' eyes that it was to be used to buy votes and take money away from the people they say they are helping.

As trade was evolving, all the creation of goods was primarily in a flat or horizontal structure or curve. That is, a man plants and produces his goods without the help or the need to buy from someone else. This is to say, goods that are produced are done entirely by an individual.

While here, we are starting to see the second level of go-betweens who facilitate the availability of various products to a broader group of people. With this, the beginning of a vertical economic structure, where people would create a product that is used in the production of another product, which is further used in another product's creation, etc., is observed. As with all societies, there is a need for value creation, addition, preservation, and protection. Even so, the need for value protection takes center stage, leading to the birth of some form of police or army protection meant to protect those who create the goods or value from theft.

To support these forces, society imposes a tax on those who create or supply services. This tax is in the form of some percentage of the value of the goods or services supplied. More so, these taxes, for the most part, were directly passed on to the end consumer. But, to note is also the fact that the producer of the goods was the primary consumer of them, meaning that he was the main provider of the tax.

In the end, the final consumer marks the point where tax money gets collected even though the producer of the goods is their primary consumer. In many economies, in fact, all of them, the one that buys last pays for all the taxes. Producers of goods are in the habit of passing tax expenses down to consumers through the inclusion of the mark-up in their product pricing. The final consumer is the one that always pays.

If you take a hard look at this discussion, you will start to see that all taxes are paid at the time of consumption. And, lower economic classes consume the most significant percentage of their income, meaning that, based on their income, they pay the most significant percentage of taxes. On the other hand, upper economic classes tend to buy things with a longer life. Yes, they buy a hamburger and eat (consume) it, but they also buy cars, homes, and other things that are not consumed immediately. Therefore, they do not quickly pay the taxes on them. Also, the taxes they pay on their income and the like are passed on using the things they produce and sell to the lower class. If he, for example, makes axes, he must collect money to live on and also pay the taxes from the price of his product. This leads me to the point that when the lower economic class thinks that raising taxes on the rich helps them, they are wrong. Any rise in taxes impacts the lower class more than it does for the rich.

Unfortunately, tax collection frequently leads to greed and the taxes become exorbitant over time. Excessive taxes are the way for people in power to become rich. No matter where the tax is taken from, it is always paid by the end consumer. Those at other levels in the chain of production and delivery only accumulate the taxes they pay from the end consumer. The end consumption is where the product is destroyed through eating, going bad, deteriorating because of age, destruction due to natural forces, etc. That is when the product or service ceases to exist, and all value is gone.

MONEY

What is MONEY? Money is an arbitrary construct used to define the value of different items. It has no value in itself but is used to define the value relationship of different items instantaneously. There is not much of a difference between the definition of money and that of the system of numbers. The number one has no value, but it is used to represent the quantity, or amount of other things. One can represent a bushel of apples, but its only function is to differentiate between one bushel of apples and two bushels of apples. In no way does it describe the apples or the size of the bushel. It just says that there is a single bushel of apples. Money is the same. A dollar does not describe the size of the bushel of apples you are buying or the condition of the same apples. It just says the instantaneous value of the bushel of apples at hand is worth a dollar. The value of the apples is only there in the number of people it will feed and how badly they need them.

The early use of precious metals and gems was the start of money. My bushel of carrots is worth one gold ring while your bushel of apples is worth two gold rings. This concept could then be used to "value," or more accurately, give a relationship of values for the various items in trade, leading to the complication of exchange rates. For example, a diamond could be worth two gold rings or one bushel of apples. Some other people might see that relationship a little differently, leading to multiple different exchange rates for the same items.

With this added complication, some people noticed that they could manipulate the exchange rates such that they could produce a profit for themselves just from the exchange rates themselves. While this could be done, they could not create substantial exchange rate differences as the items used in exchange had an underlying intrinsic value that was hard to manipulate. Except for receipts, up to this point, all barter or exchange was done by exchanging items that had an intrinsic worth that was used to establish the exchange rate.

GOVERNMENT AND MONEY

Governments started getting involved in the exchange of goods. They started developing a form of monetary exchange based on coins of a specific weight of valuable metals. These coins had a particular intrinsic value, and again, the exchange rate stayed relatively steady. These coins made barter and exchange of value easier because everyone was using the same base for exchange. That is, you did not have to know the value difference of, say, gold vs. diamonds or gold vs. silver or silver vs. copper, etc. Everything could be done using the same base.

The government, also, started seeing that they could manipulate the exchange rate. They saw that just by defining a coin as a worth in relationship to other money, they could sell coins of lesser intrinsic value for higher worth. As governments and their politicians started seeing the flow of money from taxes, they kept wanting more. As people started to complain, the politicians started to look for different taxes so that they could keep the tax rate low for the people but the other taxes would increase the tax revenue.

This leads me to one of the first governmental tax fallacies. Virtually, all forms of tax, and at whatever level, ends up being paid by the end-user of the products or services. The person or entity paying the tax gets the money to pay the tax from his own consumption or the person buying his goods or services.

IMPACT OF TAXES

No matter how the government and the politicians try to sell the taxes, it is always the lower economic class that pays the biggest percentage of their income as taxes. As I have stated before, tax money is collected at the consumption level of any product or service. In the lower economic class, most, if not all, of the income goes to the consumption of necessities to survive. Very little is spent on long-term items that will slow the taxes down. It is almost all spent on immediate consumption and immediate application to tax.

HIERARCHICAL TAX ACCUMULATION

Unlike my earlier discussion of horizontal economic structure, the current economy is built on a vertical structure. As an example, a farmer may have grown beans for his own consumption, but he buys the seeds, the tractor to plant and harvest them; he also pays for water to water the beans, the workers to tend to them, etc. All of these hierarchical elements are taxed. And, the farmer pays for these, becoming part of his cost of doing business.

The farmer then adds his property taxes and income tax and any other taxes to his cost of doing business. He applies his percentage of profit to the total. This percentage of profit only inflates the taxes collected to this point.

The beans are picked up by a truck driver who pays gas tax, road tax, all the taxes involved in producing the truck and any taxes on any other equipment or structures he needs. Again, he adds his percentage for profit. Further inflating the taxes already collected. He takes the beans to the canning plant where the taxes paid by the employees; the taxes paid on the building and equipment as above, are added to the cost of doing business along with a percentage profit. The canned beans are then trucked to the grocery where the taxes paid by each are added to their cost of doing business. They add the cost of the can (and upstream taxes), those consumables for processing to the cost of the product. They also add their percentage profit to the ultimate selling price of the beans.

At the bottom of this production line, a consumer buys the can of beans and consumes them. At this time, all the taxes are funded, and the incremental percentages of return to the workers and businesses, too, are funded. But all this money is now destroyed as the beans no longer exist. In this hierarchical economic example, the end-user pays for all the taxes accrued. He pays for all the different entities and the inflation of them and profits caused by each incremental add of profit percentage.

All of these taxes on taxes and incremental profit percentages conspire to increase the price of the goods. This, especially, affects the lower economic class where most, if not all, of their money, is used upon the necessary consumables. More taxes at different levels and higher taxes all conspire against the poor. How can we fight a war against poverty when the government and politicians are plotting to take a larger percentage of their meager money as taxes?

We have required nutrition facts on food products. I think there should be a requirement to put the tax facts on all products showing all the taxes collected at the consumption of the product. I am talking about all the taxes, including taxes generated in construction and the interest paid on the loan for that tax.

IMAGINARY TAXES

Something that most people do not know or understand is the fact that there are two types of taxes collected. There are REAL taxes collected from the purely private sector, and there are the IMAGINARY taxes from government spending dollars. An old saying my dad had was, "You can't tax, tax." Once the money is collected as tax, you cannot gain any new tax money from it. This is similar to reaching down and grabbing your shoelaces and trying to lift yourself off the floor. It can't happen.

As an example, let's take $7,500 in taxes and send it to the IRS. The IRS records it as revenue and sends the money off to the Treasury Department. At this point, the Treasury has a balance of $7,500. Now, let's say, we need to pay a Congressman $10,000 with an expected tax rate of 25%. So, we write a check for $10,000, showing a withholding of $2,500. This withholding is reported to the IRS, who reports a revenue of $2,500. At this point, the check is deposited in the Congressman's Bank account. The IRS now says it collected a total of $10,000. The private sector reports it sent in $7,500. The Congressman's Bank reports $7,500. And the Treasury reports a balance of $0.00.

How does the IRS report $10,000 revenue collected when $7,500 came in and $7,500 went out and leaving a zero balance in the Treasury? Imaginary taxes? Actually, the $2,500 is a rebate to the Government. It is their money to start with and it ends up their money in the end. This example would work the same with $100,000 owed to the Congressman and having a 92.5% tax. The IRS would report $100,000 revenue, the Congressman would deposit $7,500 and the Treasury would report a balance of ZERO. Where did the $92,500 go?

Another thing to consider here is that the $10,000 payment and its imaginary $2,500 in "tax" is for a single payment. This may have been a monthly payment in which case the imaginary $2,500 would have been collected 12 times over the year. This means for this one person; the IRS would have said that it collected $30,000 in imaginary tax. Consider how many payments are actually being made by the government and how many imaginary dollars are being reported by the IRS? This also applies to the tax dollars spent by the recipient. Taxes on them is also imaginary.

DO THE MATH!

No matter how the government and the politicians try to hide it, there are no real taxes collected on money spent by the government. Not only at the first level but all the hands that money goes through, no real taxes! My congressman says that he pays taxes, it shows up on his check. That should be labeled as a rebate of tax money. Try paying someone in your family $100 a week and charge them $100 a week for living expenses. At the end of the year, you would have collected $5,200. Do you have $5,200 more than you would have had? Should you report this $5,200 as income and pay taxes on it?

All the taxes collected on dollars the government spent would not buy one bullet for our fighting men and women. By the way, although the math might get more complicated, the same holds true for every level of government. All levels of government, Federal, State, County, City and Local are essentially different pockets in the same coat. There is only one Government and it has many departments or divisions. The Federal Government could collect all the tax money and send it back to the individual taxing entities and we would have the same result we have now.

The politicians would like you to think that the taxing entities are separate so that the tax numbers do not look that big. Bait and Switch? All of these taxes need to be added to get the actual tax that the people are paying.

THE FALLACY OF WAGE INCREASES AND SAVINGS

MINIMUM WAGE RAISES

Arbitrary increases in pay are counterproductive. People think that, just because they will receive more money or pieces of paper to do the same job at the same level, they are making more money! Unless the pay raise is for higher production value, the value of the increase is actually diminished. The perceived raise is actually a loss in value for the people! I have a "Remember When" card from 1943. It says that in 1943, the average income was $2,041.00 per year. A new house cost $3,600.00 back then, and sugar was $0.75 for 10 pounds. Coffee was retailing at $0.46 per pound.

Now, consider those same items today. For example, looking at an advertisement at the time of writing, Maxwell House coffee was selling for $6.49 per 30.6oz, which translates to $2.55 a pound. If you have a card and a coupon, you can get it for $4.99, which is still $1.96 a pound. Why is a pound of coffee now worth $1.96? What makes it so valuable? Is it that much better than before? None of the above. That value of that pound of coffee is still the same as it was. It will still make the same number of cups of coffee. Its value has not changed, but it's worth has. Worth is the dollar value placed on the item relative to the worth (not value) of other items.

Worth is a relative measure where value is more a constant, as reflected in the number of cups of coffee it will make. Worth is not only the relationship with other items, but it is also what people are willing to pay for the item or what people are ready to sell the item for. For example, if there is an excess of the item available, it's worth might be less. Conversely, if there is a shortage of the item, it's worth might be more. In either case, the value of the item is not changed, only the worth.

Another factor to worth is how much the average person is making. As the average person's wages for the same value output goes up, so will the cost of all items. This will then increase the worth of items, but again, it will not increase the value of those items. Along with the increase in worth of things, there are many other factors caused by just paying people more for the same job and the same output.

A minimum wage increase eventually causes the pay for all jobs to be re-evaluated. People will be demanding, and deserving pay increases to compensate for the minimum wage increase.

Take the guy flipping hamburgers at McDonald's for minimum wage and the person working at the window serving the food and collecting the money. The guy flipping hamburgers has a particular task that does not require a lot of thought to do. The person working at the window has many tasks involved with getting the food to the people. That person also had the added responsibility of correctly collecting the money and giving the proper change. One job does not have a lot of responsibility, while the other has much more responsibility. That is why the person working the window should and will be paid more. The problem comes when the minimum wage raise goes in; this raises the hamburger flippers pay to equal or greater than the person working the window. Therefore, the wage of the window person must also go up.

This will work its way through all wage levels causing everyone's wage (worth) to go up, but this does not increase the value of their work. The fact that the value does not increase causes inflation. Now that we have established the fact that all wages will eventually go up, we need to consider the tax consequences. This upward movement of wages will move people into higher tax brackets, causing them to pay a bigger percentage of their dollars in taxes. And, in the end, it is the government that benefits the most out of it.

So, when wages rise together with tax, the worth of all the items they buy will also go up proportional to the minimum wage increase. The result is that without the tax increase, the relative value of their income will not change. With the tax increase included, the relative value of their income will go down. Along with this reduction, many people getting some form of government or private assistance may see their dollar pay go up past the threshold to qualify for government assistance programs. This causes them to lose their eligibility for these programs and the value they were receiving in the first place.

Now that we have discussed some of the more obvious but damaging results of a minimum (or any) wage raise. We need to focus on some of the less obvious but more damaging aspects of non-value-added wage increases. Back in the 1920s or 30s, a hamburger meal was around $0.15. If we could go back and put $0.15 and that hamburger meal under the mattress, which would be worth more today? (O.K. some of you are thinking the hamburger would be no good, but it is just for the example.) The hamburger meal would be worth more, but its value has not changed. The problem is that the value of the money has decreased while the value of the hamburger stayed the same, and people deemed that it was worth more.

This shows that the value represented by money and any "dollar" denominated instruments will decrease in value as the general, non-value increased, wages are raised. As an example, where I live, the minimum wage was raised from roughly $8.00 to $12.00 over roughly 4 years. (You can use your own numbers if you wish.) If you wanted to save 12 hours of work for use in the future, you would put $8.00 times 12 hours in the bank. This would be $96.00. Four years later, if you wanted to use those 12 hours to buy something and you would find that you only have 8 hours of value in the bank. 8 hours times $12.00 per hour equals $96.00 that you put away. You have lost the value of 4 hours' worth of work.

While you are now making more dollars at minimum wage, you might have lost to taxes, and in some cases, you might have lost government assistance too. Your savings and the money in your wallet could not be speared also.

Not only are your savings hit, but many of you have retirement plans and/or Social Security. Wage raises heavily impact these. There are your own retirement plans, company plans, state plans, federal plans, military plans, etc. All of these plans were built and funded by putting a portion of your hours worked, in the form of dollars, away. There are tables and formulas that determine how much is needed to be put away to pay out a given amount when you retire. These tables and formulas are based on current conditions and do not include the unknown of the future.

I have seen numbers of 10-20 trillion dollars of unfunded government liability. A large portion of that, I think, is unfunded retirement. Why is so much unfunded? Let's look at what happens when we do an arbitrary wage increase from $8.00 to $12.00. The social security trust fund has several trillion dollars in it. Let's look at just one trillion dollars and what happens to that. One trillion dollars is equivalent to 125 billion hours of work saved at $8.00 per hour. So, they could pay out 125 billion hours at $8.00 to retirees. Now, let's see what happens when we move the wage to $12.00. A trillion dollars will pay out 83.3 billion equivalent hours of work. This is a loss of 41.7 billion hours needed to be paid out. At the $12 wage rate, this means that they need to add $500.4 billion dollars to every trillion dollars in the trust fund just to put it back to the same level of support before the wage increase.

This must be considered as the destruction of $500.4 billion dollars. The value of the dollars in these trust funds was decreased by that amount. This is like manipulating the exchange rate between countries. We know that with the wage increase, the amount withheld and paid for Social Security will also go up. The problem is that this increase is only to cover the required deposits as if the trust fund was fully funded for the current wage rates. But it does not cover any of the $500.4 billion per trillion that is needed to make these retirement funds whole again.

In the case of the government, it implies that they will have to raise taxes to cover that amount. Again, the people that had a raise will now be paying higher taxes (or more money into their retirement accounts) just to re-establish their base instead of enjoying the money. Some people will say that growth in investment will take care of that. But, the investment growth was figured into the initial funding requirements and is there either way and in no way affects the $500.4 billion per trillion number.

Social security trust fund is 2.9 trillion dollars				
				(Shortage Dollars)
Minimum wage		Saved Hours	Saved Hours Lost	At Minimum Wage
$8.00	2,900,000,000,000	362,500,000,000	0	$0
$9.00	2,900,000,000,000	322,222,222,222	-40,277,777,778	-$362,500,000,000
$10.00	2,900,000,000,000	290,000,000,000	-72,500,000,000	-$725,000,000,000
$11.00	2,900,000,000,000	263,636,363,636	-98,863,636,364	-$1,087,500,000,000
$12.00	2,900,000,000,000	241,666,666,667	-120,833,333,333	-$1,450,000,000,000
$13.00	2,900,000,000,000	223,076,923,077	-139,423,076,923	-$1,812,500,000,000
$14.00	2,900,000,000,000	207,142,857,143	-155,357,142,857	-$2,175,000,000,000
$15.00	2,900,000,000,000	193,333,333,333	-169,166,666,667	-$2,537,500,000,000

Consider the fact that about 40% of the base Trust Funds disappeared in those four years. With the Trust Fund money earning 2-3% interest and intended to keep the fund growing in a static economy, where is the roughly 10% needed to cover the destruction coming from? Also, as soon as the increase in the minimum wage is completed, people will start trying to initiate another round of increases to make up for the extra taxes they will have to pay to correct the shortage, and the cycle goes round and round.

The more we make arbitrary wage increases, be it by government setting higher minimum wages or Union or Associations getting higher wages for the same job, the more value we are destroying. Some years ago, during the political campaign season, one or the other party was blaming the other for pushing Grandma and Grandpa off of the cliff. I remember seeing cartoons of people in wheelchairs being forced off of the cliff. These arbitrary wage increases are what is pushing them off of the cliff.

Many retired people have bonds, certificates of deposit, and annuities, etc. These are all dollar-denominated instruments of finance. The same ratio of destruction of the value of these, as seen in the above example, will apply. These people will find that the money they thought they had will not buy as much or go as far as they thought when they put it away. All of these examples show that these increases have a very devastating effect on the lower economic class. There is no way around that as long as we keep arbitrarily raising wages.

On the flip side, many people in the mid to upper economic classes are aware of this and have found ways not only to mitigate this problem for themselves but to profit from these increases.

I, myself, have seen some of my investments yield a small profit from these increases. I suppose I should be happy about that. I have mixed emotions about it. Yes, I like the extra profit for myself, but, on the other hand, I see the future problems for the lower-income classes as well as the potential devastation this could eventually cause to the overall economy.

Just remember, the money lost in these investments is not really lost. It tends to move from the lower-income classes to the upper-income class. In the end, it is the former who are providing more dollars that are widening the divide between the poor and the rich. Be careful of what you wish for; it may turn around and bite you! We all need to understand how this works and DO THE MATH. If we don't, we will be like Greece and other countries that have had to make massive changes to their economy or those that have gone bankrupt. These problems are not trivial and need us all to understand them.

PAYING PEOPLE WHAT THEY NEED

At this point, I reiterate my prior position that people must not be paid because of what they feel they are entitled to. But, the value that they add to the firm is the one that must be rewarded. My grandmother worked in a button factory, and her salary was based on piecework. She had a knack for work and was very coordinated while using the button machine. She was always ahead of the machine, and had the foreman raise the speed of her machine because it was slowing her down. This meant that she was able to produce more buttons per hour, therefore increasing her piecework pay per hour.

Other workers were very upset that she was making more money per hour than they were. They felt that they needed the money as badly as she did. They protested to the foreman about the discrepancy in pay. The foreman told them that when they could produce as many good pieces per hour as she had been producing, then he would increase the speed of their machines too. It was not how fast the machines were, but how much good product they produced at any given speed of the machine.

Even though they may have felt that they needed more pay, the company could not pay more for more rejected material. The salary for those jobs was based on the value produced. No company can stay in business paying for poor value. The true question as to what people need comes down to who is going to determine what a person needs. If it is the politicians and government, it is going to end up a one size fits all. This means that some people will get much more than they need, and others will get much less than they need.

Also, with this approach, the value produced by the people will not be taken into account. Meaning that a person who produces a lot will be expected to continue at that level of production while others start producing less and still claim their needs are higher. Pretty soon, the producers will stop producing as much, and there will not be enough production to support those who do not deliver. The economy, as has been shown time and again, will collapse. Look at history!

Paying a person based on what they need is a form of Socialism. And one of the biggest flaws of socialism is that it will only work until the OTHER person's money runs out. And the more they need, the quicker the other person's money runs out.

BUYING SUPPORT WITH YOUR MONEY

All of these things allow people to buy your support and votes with "YOUR" money!

Politicians, well-meaning people, and organizations all have found that by telling people that they are going to get them more money, healthcare, or other forms of support for "free," they would get their support and even votes. What they do not tell you, and many do not understand, it that it is "YOUR" money that is actually going to pay for those items. A raise without corresponding increase in the value of production only destroys the value of your savings, retirement, and the money in your pocket! So, right off the bat, they are buying your vote with your money by destroying some of its value while making you think they are helping you!

Now there is the loss of value in bonds, CD's, bank accounts, annuities, dollars in your pocket, etc. To put the value of these items back to what it was before the wages increase, you will have to come up with an amount of money equal to the percentage increase in wages. This will only put it back to the value before the wage increase. When it comes to government plans such as Social Security, government employee retirement plans, and the like, this shortage will have to be made up from taxes of some sort. Now, as

MISUNDERSTOOD MONEY

we know, government employees and people receiving government assistants do not pay real taxes, all of this money will have to come from the private sector, meaning a double whammy on their taxes. They will have to not only raise their prices to cover the cost of the wage increase but also, they will have to raise their prices to cover the increased taxes.

The biggest problem with this is that the end consumers will pay this increased cost (and taxes). What group of people are these end consumers? These are all the people that buy products that they entirely use up. For example, you buy a hamburger and eat it, you have consumed the product, and it does not exist anymore. At this point, you have paid all the taxes that have been incurred all the way through the creation of that hamburger. You are the end consumer and you pay the taxes.

Now, the upper classes buy and invest in a lot of things, as well as their hamburger. Nevertheless, at day's end, they still have many of the things that they have bought. They did consume the hamburger and paid the taxes on it, but they haven't completely consumed all of the items they bought, so the taxes are still waiting to be collected on them.

Many in the classes that all these do-gooders (they are trying to do something good but they have not done the math) are trying to help are basically living hand to mouth. All the money they make goes into buying things that they immediately consume. This group of people is paying the biggest percentage of their money in immediate taxes! Because these taxes, throughout the process, will have gone up to make up the deficits, this class will be paying for the purchase of the votes to get a pay raise.

While many of these people, groups, organizations, politicians, etc., genuinely believe they are helping people make more value to make their life easier, they need to do the math to see what they are actually doing to the people. As I have said, multitudes are trying to help people, but many know the math and are using this to gain power and votes regardless of the damage they are doing to people.

I was a member of one of the senior associations that were backing the minimum wage increase to help the seniors who had to work and make more value. I tried to point out to them that they were actually hurting the seniors. They responded that it was their position, and they were going to stick with it. Any argument that I tried to present as the damage fell on deaf ears and was ignored. Here again, is a group selling the people that they are helping them to make more to buy their support.

Another thing to consider is that, as the tax percentage that the lowest income class is paying goes up, they have less value to purchase life-sustaining needs. At some point, the amount they have left, after paying any direct and indirect taxes, is not enough to sustain life. This is when people start dropping out of the economy, and we see a spike in people living on the streets, in the parks, etc.

MONEY: HOW ABOUT INTRODUCING A NEW STANDARD OF MEASURE?

People, for a long time, have attached the value of money on various items. Maybe it is time to look at a different base for money or exchange medium. The US Dollar has been based, at times, on Gold or Silver. Politicians and the people could not manipulate the value as they would have liked, so they dropped those as a base. Many countries and exchange mediums are not based on anything of value. Take the bitcoin craze, for example. What stationary item is it based on? Nothing that I know of. Therefore, in my opinion, it is nothing more than a Ponzi scheme.

In Ponzi schemes, the first people in make a lot of money off entrants that join afterward. But eventually, less people would be coming in to join the scheme, resulting in huge losses, especially on the late entrants. It is a bit like socialism; it works until the others' money runs out. I might suggest that instead of the dollar, which is not really based on anything, we consider the MWH.

What is the MWH? You may be asking. Well, It is a medium of exchange based on one Minimum Wage-Hour. A minimum wage hour would be equivalent to a person working one hour at an entry-level job in the fast-food industry. Such as a person requiring very little training to stand at a grill and flipping hamburgers. Based on this hour of work, the person taking orders and handling the money, who would be considered more skilled, would be paid a percentage point(s) more than one MWH.

Eventually, the pay for all jobs would be based on the MWH. Basically, this is how the pay scale for jobs will be determined. What is the value of a particular job and the hour of production produced?

In this day, our major problem, especially when discussing these topics, is that the Politicians, Governments, Unions, etc., all think that one person or job should be paid more, not for what they produce, but for what they need. If the pay for all jobs was based on the pay for a minimum wage-hour, the pay scales would stabilize. Meaning that, when you put one MWH hour away in your retirement account, you would get one MWH back along with any accrued interest. This would be an improvement over having the minimum wage go from $8 to $12 an hour. With this increase, when you put 12 minimum wage hours away at the start, you will only have 8 minimum wage hours that you can take out. That is ignoring the interest, which is far outpaced by the increases.

INTERSTATE EXCHANGE RATE

With the various States setting different minimum wage rates and the Unions establishing arbitrary wage rates in different industries, something must be done to level the field between states. For example, teachers, especially in New York City, make a lot more money than those in, say Arizona, New Mexico, Arkansas, or Iowa. The problem is, people only look at the dollars made. Those teachers in New York City, with its higher cost of living, actually make less value than those in the other states. Teachers in New York City make far less than is needed to buy a home or rent an apartment. Where the teachers in those other states are much closer to affording the type of home they want.

This problem is explained by the relative cost of living in various locations. But, just using the cost of living to explain the difference does not help anyone. This problem is also seen in the purchasing of items from the high cost of living states as opposed to low cost of living states. Many companies have moved from the high-cost states to lower-cost states so that they can keep the costs down to allow people in the lower-cost states to afford their products.

It might be best for the various states to establish their own currency. This way, the market could then establish an exchange rate for the currency of one state over the other. While this approach would create many problems of its own, it could help to level the playing field for all the people.

Another item that makes the cost of living in some states higher than in other states is taxes. The amount, no, not the amount, but the percentage of taxes taken from the economy also affects the cost of living in the various states. With a higher percentage of taxes, the cost of living also goes up.

Why do some states have higher taxes than in others? Mostly because of political spending. All of the states have some basic requirements for taxes. These include the safety provided by the police and fire departments. Legal recourse provided by the courts. The need for roads and infrastructure to facilitate businesses that produce jobs. And also needed is education for the people.

These are the basic needs that apply equally to the citizens of the state. Beyond that are the things that can be best handled by the people and organizations. The problem is that the politicians need money for political needs of the state. The more the politicians have the state doing things that are better provided by the private sector, the more they need taxes.

They say the people need housing. But housing comes from working hard and earning a living, including working with family members to achieve this. Higher education can be achieved with hard work and effort too. But not everyone will gain from higher education. Many people are gifted in jobs that do not require higher education. We need plumbers, mechanics, and garbage collectors. There are those that have talent and enjoy these jobs. They do not need a college degree for these jobs. Some might need specific training but not the expense of a college education.

Healthcare need not be as expensive as it is. This is caused by two major factors: The vertical or hierarchical structure needed to provide health care. This structure and the high paying jobs needed cause the amount of tax collected to be quite high. The second is the legal system that the state is allowing. I agree people should be compensated for damages caused. But, the amount of compensation should not be excessive. There was a case where someone spilled a hot cup of coffee and got a million-dollar award. Excessive? The other part is the punitive damage awards. This is supposed to be punishment for the damages that were or might have been done to other people. As this is supposed to be for damages to other people, this money should be collected by the state to give everyone a little relief for their damages.

As has been discussed, politicians tend to be in support of giving the people what they think they need, instead of letting the people get the rewards for what they produce.

LEGAL THEFT

The legal system and the awards they are getting are now out of hand. A million-dollar award for spilling a hot cup of coffee on one's self, for example, does not make sense at all. People complain about the high cost of health care. The education system that produces people in the health care field is filled with highly qualified people who are well paid. They are all paying a significant tax rate, and their facilities are expensive and loaded with taxes. The direct providers of health care have paid a lot of people's taxes along the way. They must recoup that money before they can start to make money for themselves. But as they begin servicing people, their liability rises. Meaning that they must buy insurance and help pay the taxes of those involved in the insurance.

The cost of their insurance is based on the liability they may be open to. This is determined by the number of awards the legal system gives out for the various types of claims. The more the liability, the more the doctor pays for insurance. Part of the problem with liability is, it has moved from negligence to how well the lawyers can spin the doctors' attempts to help the patient, so he should have known better. The lawyers are now practicing medicine.

The doctor also has to pay for his office, any assistants or help he has. All of these involve accumulated taxes that they have paid and will have to pay. These all add to the costs a doctor must pay before he can make a living. We have all heard about the student loan problem. With doctors, they have huge sums of student loans (to pay the taxes of those institutions he attended). Starting out, he must pay the large payments on these loans. This means he must have a substantial income as he develops his practice. These loans, however, disappear over time.

Some would say that he should lower his rates as he pays them off. The problem would be that the competition for patients tends to attract patients to established doctors and away from new practices due to the lower prices. It makes it impossible for new doctors to succeed.

PILLS TAXES AND LIABILITY

Another thing that makes Healthcare so expensive is the cost of medicines. The development of drugs and medical equipment takes a lot of time and a lot of work by many highly skilled people. Most of these people are in higher tax brackets, so a good percentage of their pay goes to paying their taxes. This money is eventually paid by the end-users of the equipment or medicines they produce - (YOU!)

While this development is taking place, the company is investing the money to carry out the development. This money does not make money until the product goes to market. This may take up to tens of years. So, all of this time, the company is investing money in hopes of getting a return. Not only are they investing the money, but they are losing the opportunity to get an immediate return by investing elsewhere. All of the costs and "time value" of money they have invested need to be recouped when the product goes to market.

When the product is ready to go to market, many things must be considered in establishing the selling price of the product. First, there is the problem of how long the product will last on the market before something new and better replaces it. This means that is the time to recoup their investments. The aim is to get a reasonable return on investment as well as covering their taxes on the sales. They also must estimate how many units will be sold or consumed over that period of time.

Now they must look at the liability that they might encounter with the use of their product. With the lawyers using the liability laws like the lottery and seeking ever higher awards for their clients, this can be a huge number. If they figure the potential liability too low, they stand the chance of bankrupting the company and putting all the employees out of jobs. They must balance that with the resulting cost of the product.

They must also consider the carrying costs of the money they have invested and yet to recoop. They then take all the resulting cost estimates and divide them up over the number of units that they expect to sell.

As you can see, there are two major components of the cost that do not add to the final value of the product. These are the accumulated taxes that are paid by the company, either directly or indirectly, through its employees' salaries, over the time of development, as well as the estimated potential liability for the use of the product. Neither of these huge costs adds value to the product, and are an overhead cost that each user must pay. For some products, these become the major component of the price you pay.

RICH PEOPLE AND MONEY

Back in the 1950s, the Walt Disney Studios put out a lot of cartoons featuring Mickey Mouse, Donald Duck, Goofy, and the like. One prominent character was Scrooge McDuck. He was a wealthy person and had a giant vault filled with coins and paper money. He was frequently shown diving into this collection and swimming through it like a swimming pool.

Unfortunately, this implanted the idea that rich people kept all their money in a vault, which is quite far from the truth. While a few wealthy people keep their money in more static funds, most of them invest their money in things that produce value.

I have frequently heard the phrase "you have to spend money to make money." This is far from being correct. The Government seems to think this is true and continually tries to fix things by spending money. Government spending money only destroys it. Also, the politicians seem to believe that the Government is the source of money, so they like to spend it.

The proper thing is to "invest" money to make money. People find an idea for a product or service and invest money to develop the concept. The hope is that the plan will generate sales to other people and, therefore, produce a profit for those who had the idea.

A good example is Bill Gates. He did not invent the computer but saw the need for a simple operating system that people could easily use to get value from their computers. He and some friends invested time and money to develop this "operating system."

As more and more people saw the value in the system and purchased it for their own use, the company started making a profit. This profit was then used to expand the development and functionality of the system. It required more people to help with the development and maintenance of the system, thus creating jobs for many other people.

Not only did it create direct jobs within the company, but the sales and installation of the product also developed new posts in computer stores and repair shops all across the country and world.

With all of these jobs created, there were many thousands of indirect jobs created. People in housing, food, home goods, Doctors, automobiles, mechanics, and others were all indirectly created to provide for those people in jobs he created.

The company multiplied and the "value" of the company also grew quite rapidly. Much of the value came from the growing physical plants and equipment to produce the products. (This value was not a lot of coins and paper money laying in some vault.) This gave the initial investors a sizable return on their investments.

The returns allowed the company to invest in other ideas and products, which increased their sales and value. A small return on many millions of transactions creates a substantial return to the investors, as Mr. Gates and other original investors held small investments that became very large as the company grew were. This is where he and others ended up with billions of dollars of investments (not cash, investments that grow).

People seem to think he should not have that value. One thing they do not understand is that the investment is in the company. This is a company with thousands of direct jobs and created opportunities for many more people outside of the company.

If the major holders of the company were to sell off all of the equipment, buildings, and property to convert their investments to cash (as Scrooge McDuck had) what would happen to all those direct and indirect jobs that they had created?

Thousands upon thousands of people would no longer have an income. With that many people out of jobs, the economy would slow down, and other people not directly involved with their products would lose jobs also. With that many people suddenly out of a job, there would not be enough jobs in other sectors to take up those out of a job.

The question now becomes, should the Government start taking the money away from these people? To take the "money," these people would have to start selling things off and eliminating jobs. This brings me back to an old nursery rhyme that discussed the killing of the goose that laid the golden eggs. They killed the goose to see where the golden eggs came from, but at that point, there were no more golden eggs.

If we keep attacking the rich entrepreneurs for their wealth, are we not doing the same thing? Trying to kill the golden goose to get to his golden eggs?

There was an article on FOXNEWS.COM (10/27/2014) that stated the following;

> "At a democratic rally Friday in Massachusetts, Hillary Clinton's attempt to attack 'trickle-down economics,' resulted in a spectacularly odd statement, according to The Washington Free Beacon.
>
> Clinton defended raising the minimum wage saying, 'Don't let anybody tell you that raising the minimum wage will kill jobs; they always say that.'
>
> She went on to state that businesses and corporations are not the job creators of America. 'Don't let anybody tell you that it's corporations and businesses that create jobs.' The former Secretary of State said."

The question becomes, Did Bill Gates and his associates create all of those jobs, or did the Government create them? Also, as discussed elsewhere, does the minimum wage help or hurt people in the lower class as well as all of everyone's retirement funds? I have, for years, been told that my ideas are wrong. I think there is enough here to say who is wrong and who is right.

Let's see a little more about how many rich people became wealthy. Let's use a doctor, for example. A doctor spends a lot of money and time getting his education and probably has a massive amount of student loans to pay for this education. If he is a specialist, the expense/loan is perhaps even greater.

Now the doctor is ready to open an office for his practice. The building or rented space costs him money; the equipment costs him money. He probably has to borrow money to secure these things as well as needing funding to pay for a nurse and any other help he needs.

All of this adds to the amount of money he owes! The payments on these loans are more than likely very large. He has to take these amounts and add them to electricity, water, gas, etc. Now he must figure in his liability insurance fees. After all the expenses are calculated, he then adds an amount for his pay or return on his investment. This amount is then broken down by hours of operation or number of patients he plans to see. As you should be able to see, this is a huge number, but it is not excessive given what he has to pay back and pay for his help.

In the beginning, he will have to conserve and work hard to cover his costs. As time goes by and he is able to reduce his debt, he will start making more money for himself. He may even be able to see more patients who will increase his profit after expenses.

At this point, people might say he should also cut his prices. Well, if he does that, other doctors trying to start will be at a disadvantage because they will not be able to compete with his prices. This means if all the well-established doctors cut their prices there would be no incentive for new doctors to go into practice, thus creating a doctor shortage.

Another way to look at it is if the doctor is not making a sufficient percentage of profit, no bank or lending agency will be willing to lend him money if he needs to buy new equipment or office space.

He may be able to bring in other doctors from whom he can collect rent on the space and equipment. By leveraging his assets in this way, he can make more than he can by himself. All of this leads to him making more than many other people. He did not do it by stealing from anyone; he did it by wise investments.

Many rich people got there through hard work and wise investments. The same opportunity everyone has if they choose to understand the process and can find a product that people want.

LET THE OTHER GUY PAY FOR IT

It appears that people think that having someone else pay for their things helps them. While this may be true in some isolated instances, in most cases, it is the opposite that is true.

Let's start off with a simple concept, the cash back credit card or the website that will get you cash back on your online purchases. The idea they promote is that someone else will give you free money, the other guy will pay for it.

First of all, the fundamental credit card costs the business money to have someone else collect the money from you and give it to them. They must pay the credit card company or clearinghouse to process the money. That is the concept, but that is not accurate. The business does not pay them to handle the money; YOU pay for it at higher prices. The only place a company gets its money is from its customers, YOU.

So, in actuality, you are paying for all the people that process the credit card transactions. This is usually in the 1 to 2% range. You are paying an extra 1% to 2% on your purchases for the privilege of using some other companys' card.

I am not saying that there isn't any advantage to the merchant. The fact that they do not have lots of cash at the end of the day that they must take to the bank or worry about having a robbery and losing the money, can be a plus. Also, this can help in other ways to make bookkeeping easier for the business.

Now that we have talked about the basics of credit card transactions, let's include the cashback or as some ads have said: "the money you make for using their card." Again, the money is coming from you. The card companies raise the fee to the merchant to cover the cost of the cashback plus an additional fee for processing and re-paying some of your money to you. So, if you are using one of those 5% cashback cards, you are not only paying the original 1%-2% card fee, but you must add the 5% cashback and the fees to process that. This means that, instead of paying the extra 1% to 2% for the service fee, you are now paying a 6% to 8% premium, for the products you are buying, to get 5% back.

Not only are you paying the card company a substantial fee, but they must also have a high enough fee to pay for all the advertising to mention to you that you are "making" money using their card. In fact, the extra charge is raising the price of the goods and adding to inflation, which makes your dollar less valuable. That is, the value of your dollar goes down because you are getting less value for it.

Recently, I heard that the CEO of a major bank wants the country to do away with cash. Yes, it costs them a little more to handle the small percentage of cash (compared to their overall dollar amount) that the people bring in. On the other hand, if instead of passing cash from one person to another or business, people were to use their credit cards, they could make the extra fees. Consider how many times cash changes hands without the bank or card companies being involved? All of these transactions are done without them collecting their 2%. That adds up to a lot of money they do not get their hands on!

Another problem, or advantage, depending on who you are and which way you look at it, is that without cash, all transactions will have an electronic record somewhere. With these electronic records and all the A.I. computers, the Government will be able to track your every move. As with any government, it will depend on who is in control. For example, Hitler and the Third Reich would love to have had that kind of access to information about people.

People seem to want to buy into the fact that someone else is paying for it. Nowhere else can this be seen better than in the government and its politicians!

Many of them seem to think that the government should spend tax dollars on all sorts of things. They believe that someone else that is paying is the government. The government has no money! The only place that they get their money is from the people! And not all the people do pay these taxes – at least in real terms. Only those in the private sector do pay real taxes. Those people receiving any form of money from the government are only giving the government back a refund of some of the money the government gave them.

Many politicians want to put more and more people on welfare. They want the government to pay for it. The government has no money of its own, so they cannot pay for it. The only place the money comes from is the private sector taxpayers. So, if you are a private-sector taxpayer, you are the other guy that is paying for it. No one in the public sector is helping you out.

Let's take the example that assumes that everyone is put on welfare. Let's assume that they pay 10% "tax" (refund to be given back to them in the next cycle) on their income. You have 100% less the 10% refund they return, leaving 90% of their welfare check that needs to be paid. As, at this point, there are no private-sector taxpayers left, there is no money to pay them with! This is a simple fact of most, if not all, socialist ideas of the government paying for everything that it only works until the OTHER person's money runs out.

Government-run health insurance or health benefits is another similar problem where they think that as long as the other person is paying for it, they do not have to worry about it. This presents the same problem as putting everyone on welfare. The more people that are on the program, the less real money the government has to pay for it.

Given the fact that no government spending produces real tax money and at that, is only a small percentage of the cost of the programs, this will only work until the other people run out of money. You might argue that the fees paid for being on the plan pay for the services. Any money collected by the government is similar to taxes levied by the government. The only real fees come from the private sector. If everyone is on the plan, there will be no private sector to pay for it. It only works until the other person's money runs out!

In all of this, I am not saying that there are not legitimate programs and expenses of the government. Our founding fathers enumerated many of them when they wrote the constitution. Some of them like the main branches of the government, the military, postal roads, and the like. I do not see where they said everyone should have a free ride paid for by the government. I think that they understood that affected people as a group and not those things that affect people individually were to be taken care of by the government. I think they realized that those kinds of endeavors only work until the other person runs out of money.

Public housing is another project that only works until the other person's money runs out. Why do so many people need help with health insurance, welfare, public housing, etc? One of the main reasons is that government taxes, at all levels, are taking so much money from the private sector that there is not enough to pay the lower class a decent wage—a wage that will cover all the taxes and other mandated expenses that a person has.

Remember, a person pays Federal taxes, State taxes, Local taxes, sales taxes, transfer taxes, and on and on. Not only do they pay these directly for the things they consume. They are paying these taxes for all the people up-stream in the production of the products they buy and consume. It is no wonder that so many people are having a hard time, and as the Government and the Politicians keep trying to do more, there will be more people in financial trouble.

While we are on the subject of pay, the "gross" pay that people receive from businesses is not the total payment they receive. One example is the portion of the social security tax that the businesses pay. This is actually part of the pay as far as the company is concerned, but it does not show up on the paycheck. If you include this and other expenses the company has because it has that employee, the amount of "tax" the people pay is even larger than suggested above.

We are going to find that there is a limit to all these taxes and mandated expenses. The problem is when we hit that limit, the other people will be out of money, and the economy will collapses as it has done in other countries that have not paid attention to these problems.

If you look hard at all those socialistic and communistic ideas, I think you will see that they all are based on the Government taking care of the people's problems. Just remember, there is really no such thing as Government when it comes to money. The money always comes from the private sector. To say the Government is going to pay for it is to say that the people in the private sector are going to pay for it. With the socialists and communists, they want to have everything run by the Government; therefore, there will be no private sector to pay for it. Where do they think the money will come from?

GOVERNMENTS: PRODUCTION AND ALLOCATIVE EFFICIENCY

By definition, politics is about determining who gets what, at what time, and in what quantity. But, are governments good at doing this job? If they are good at it, we say they are productive and allocative efficient; if not, well, the opposite holds.

But first, to get everyone on the same page, let's explain Efficiency Experts. There is a college curriculum that includes methods improvement, time study, etc. This is called Industrial Engineering. A lot of which is common sense along with looking at the things that affect the methods improvement as well as those things the improvement will affect. A trained Industrial Engineer will have been trained to look further than the process at hand.

On the other hand, the Efficiency Experts, while using common sense, will tend to focus on a particular problem and try to solve it with no concept of what else is involved.

A plant I worked at made aluminum windows. Along with these windows were the screens that went on the windows. The bosses decided that they wanted to control the cost of those screens and decided they wanted to put the assembly of those frames on a piece work basis. They took the Efficiency Expert approach and watched how many the person produced in a given length of time. They figured that the person costs about ten cents a frame to assemble them. From this limited information, they set the piece work standard at ten cents with no strings attached. The assembler, being a bit crafty, started assembling 4 or 5 frames at a time. There was nothing to say that this was not the way to do it. This caused a problem with other employees because that assembler was making 3-5 times as much as other people in the plant.

This is a perfect example of an Efficiency Expert. The Industrial Engineer would have time-studied the operation. They would have described the methods used and established a rate for that method. Any variation to that method would nullify the rate and caused a new time study to determine the proper rate.

Now that we have determined what an efficiency expert does in business let's look at what they do in Government.

In my area, the State decided to replace street signs because someone did not like how they looked. This also happened at the Federal level as politicians wanted all signs to use the same font and style.

The problem is that when the original signs were budgeted for, they were expected to last 20 to 30 years. This would mean that the cost to the taxpayer would be distributed over that period. What is not considered is that if they are being replaced sooner than the budgeted time, the remaining value of the signs must be added to the cost of the new signs to account for the costs accurately. Not only that, in any process, there is what is called a setup cost. This setup cost is usually relatively high compared to the overall cost. So, the cost of the crew and materials to go out and install the new signs without amortizing it over the true-life expectancy is quite high. Just to think about it, try replacing those signs every month and look at the cost of installing them compared to the cost of the signs.

Let us not forget that all of these costs come out of tax money paid by the private sector people. Also, none of the money spent on the installation or the materials will generate any "new" tax revenue. That money just came out of the treasury and was returned to the treasury as a rebate, not money that could be used for something else. It just keeps going in and out of the treasury.

We can take a look at this from a different angle. The various levels of government are using bonds to raise money. These bonds have numerous payback lives, meaning the taxpayers will be expected to continue to pay the bond off over that period. While this can be beneficial for major projects that have an estimated long life longer than the bond life. Things like dams and major road construction are high dollar items that have an expected long life. The problem comes when the Politicians start using the bonds as a form of revenue.

They start using bonds to pay for things with a shorter expected life than the things they are funding. I have heard, for example, people touting the need for school bonds, and they are talking about things like busses and other equipment that does not have an expected life as long as the bonds. They even talk about the need impacting the people's pay, which is an immediate consumption of the money. This means the taxpayer will be paying for years on something that will no longer exist. It is like an old saying "paying for a dead horse."

Like the example of the street signs, if the items the bond money is used for do not last as long as the bond, you end up paying for the item multiple times at the same time. There is a little bit of "bait and switch in this." When they sell the idea of the bond, they are saying that the annual cost is a given number that does not seem like a lot. As things are used up and replaced before the bond is paid off, a new bond is put in place to pay for the replacements. Now the taxpayers are paying off two or more bonds for the same thing. This means the annual cost for these items has doubled or more. So, the taxpayer is not paying what was initially projected and is, instead, paying a multiple of that amount.

The taxpayers who are voting for bond issues need to know what the bond is for and how long it will take to pay it off. Then they need to look at the expected life of the items being purchased with the bonds to see if they will still be paying for things that do not exist when bond still does. "Paying for a dead horse!"

Another thing to watch out for is the bait and switch. Bond issuing may be targeted to pay for a legitimate long-term item, but after it is approved, some, or all of the money gets used for short term items, such as salaries and supplies. These items are used up instantaneously compared to the bond's life, which means that the taxpayer is paying for a long time on something that has not existed for a long time. There needs to be some way to control this type of usage. The taxpayer could end up making a payment for a year's salary for ten or more years while new bonds are being issued each year. Not only are you paying the same salary, but you are paying interest on it for years. The taxpayer, again, loses.

ROAD TAXES FOR ELECTRIC VEHICLES

I was discussing with a neighbor when the subject of electric vehicles and the use of the roads without paying "road tax" popped up.

It brought up an interesting thought. First, there is only ONE Government. The constitution spells out what the Federal Government should be and then gives the right and authority to the other governmental entities. I.E., State, County, City, and any other governing body. This essentially makes all governing bodies part of divisions of the same one government. Therefore, all taxes and fees collected by any taxing agency are being collected by the "ONE" government. It is like they are all part of the same coat; only they each have their own pockets.

All these various taxes collected by the various taxing agencies could all be collected as a single tax on the people and then divvied up depending on various uses. One of the advantages of these various divisions is that they all collect relatively small amounts at different times so that the overall real tax that is paid does not show up as a huge sum. And all of the taxes collected are only really funded when an item is consumed.

Back to the road tax: I pointed out to my neighbor that he should look at his electric bill and see all the taxes and fees the various governing bodies put on the usage of electricity. This is essentially the road tax money paid by the electric vehicle owners. The problem people have is that this is not called "road tax," none the less this is tax revenue that is generated by the vehicle using the roads. It is just being put into a different pocket. With that, the politicians need to find a way to separate that tax money so that it can be called and used as a road tax. Road tax and tax on electricity are both being collected by the same "government"; they are the ones that need to figure out which is which.

THE GOVERNMENT SHOULD DO MORE

Recently, I had a conversation with someone who was saying, "The government should do more." There are many low-income people and families that are struggling to make ends meet. Many of them are not succeeding in doing that. They need help, and the government should help them.

I said that it is not the government's job and it hasn't worked. They replied, "They are just not doing it right!" Well, that may be true, but for thousands of years, people have been trying to do it right, and no one has succeeded for as long as I can remember.

We have had Socialistic Governments, Communistic Governments, and combinations thereof. They all tend to succeed for a short time, but eventually, the governments collapse on themselves.

We have many examples today of governments that are going bankrupt because they tried to make the government a do all save all for the people. They are still trying to "do it right," and no one is succeeding.

They all fall due to the same fundamental problems. One of which is the fact that any government money that they spend comes only from the private sector. As they do more for one group of people, there are fewer people in the private sector to pay the bills. As I have stated elsewhere, no government spending produces new taxes or revenue for the government. "You cannot tax, tax!"

I do not care how you try to "do it right" this fundamental problem will always come back to bite you. As I have heard many times, these governmental, socialistic, or communistic types of government only succeed until "they run out of other people's money." (The private sector.)

In case you are wondering about my definition of the private sector, it is anyone working and producing, whose income is not paid for by any government or government agency. This gets harder to delineate as the government expands almost into everything. Government money buys a lot of private sector goods along with the private sector. This means that many private sector jobs are actually both private and public sector jobs. Nonetheless, it is only the private sector part of the job that qualifies as private sector money. So, even though a job or business appears to be in the private sector, it may only be partially private sector, and only that portion can be counted as the private sector. Therefore, as the government grows, the private sector shrinks as these jobs and businesses do more business with the government.

There may be a large sector of the economy that appears to be the private sector, but only a portion of it is really private sector and continually shrinking.

What does this really mean? Well, as I have stated, the only real monies the government collects come from the private sector, meaning that, for those people or businesses that are a mix of the two, the taxes collected must rise such that the private sector of the business is paying more than the company would have paid if it were totally private. This is necessary to cover for the "taxes" which are not real and are collected from the public sector portion of the business.

This also reminds me of a Ponzi scheme. The first people to start getting money and help from the government will benefit the most.

After some time with the government helping and supporting more people, the source of money gets smaller and smaller. At some point, the government runs out of other people's money, and EVERYONE suffers because there is nothing left. At this point, people will be forced to go back and start over. This happened in the Great Depression, and a lot of people got hurt.

THEY HAVEN'T DONE IT RIGHT

Recently, in discussing the minimum wage and helping the lower class, I had someone tell me that they have not done it right. My response was that they have been trying it for thousands of years, and it has not worked yet. I would think with that many people trying so many times, with that time and effort, would have produced a better result.

Something one might want to consider is that over that time, the math still has not changed, and it keeps getting in the way of them achieving their goals.

Even today, people in the lower economic classes seem to think that if they have the government do things for them, they will have more. Well, folks, I hate to burst your bubble but, the lower economic classes have and always will pay a bigger percentage of their money in taxes to pay for their "gifts."

Oh, you say, they do not pay taxes. If they purchase and consume anything, they pay all the taxes collected up to the point of consumption. These taxes, while they may be unseen by the buyer, are included in every purchase. There is no way around that fact.

People keep wanting to raise the minimum wage to help lower-income classes. What they do not realize is that I estimate 15-25% or more of that minimum wage to go towards unseen taxes. A large portion of these taxes is ultimately there to pay for the things people want the government to give the people. So, let's consider what would happen if that percentage was added to their current minimum wage. They would have more value to purchase other items of their own choosing.

Another thing to consider is the fact that part of that tax goes to pay the people who collect the tax and those who decide who best to give it to. Not only are you paying for what you are getting from the government, but you are also paying for people to collect it and tell you what is to be done with your money.

No matter how people try to get ahead by having the government do things for them, they end up paying more for someone else to tell them how their money should be spent. Even if it were possible to get everyone to agree on exactly how the money should be collected and spent, everything would be more expensive, and the lower economic class would still be the biggest loser.

To those who think that no one has done it right yet, I suggest you learn and do the math and find out how to do it right.

SIDE NOTE

Ben Franklin is quoted as saying, "Those who would give up essential Liberty, to purchase a little temporary Safety, deserve neither Liberty nor Safety." In this quote, he is saying if you give up the liberty of your money to the government to give safety to others, you will not have the freedom to control your money or the safety sought for others.

This concept has been proven over and over again throughout time. Yet many people still think that giving up control of their money will, in some way, do the miracles they wish for. When someone else has control of your money, they do what THEY want, and that is not necessarily what YOU want.

This whole concept of giving up more and more of your liberties to the people running the government has time and time again proven to be devastating to those who thought they were doing a good thing.

As far as having the government trying to help people, my Father related a story to me many years ago. It was a story about a Jewish Community near where we lived. This community would help other people out in the community.

As an example, if a business owner were on the verge of losing his business, the community would come together and help him start a new one. If this happened a second time, they would give some help to get him going again. Now, if he went broke again, the community would not help him further saying, they were not in the habit of supporting failure.

Herein lies the problem with the government. They do not have the stomach to stop supporting failure. If a person continues to fail, it is their own fault, and THEY need to do something about it, not the government or me.

Yes, some people are not as capable as others, and they do need some help. Here in the area that I live, there is an organization that helps a large number of these people. They work hard and are glad to have the chance to contribute. Between the things they sell and considerable support from many people in the area, the organization has several locations and is entirely debt free. People are willing to help people who, through no fault of their own, need help. But these same people do not want the government just to keep handing out money to those who are capable and just do not wish to make an effort.

Whenever the government gets involved in helping, there is no control over who gets what. The rules keep changing depending on who is in charge. Some people think that the government is an endless source of money to be given away. History has shown that governments run by that concept fail miserably and ultimately hurt not only those they were helping but also the private sector that was supporting the government. Take a look at the many governments that have failed and see why. Mostly they could not afford to support the number of people and projects they were trying to help.

TEACHING ABOUT MONEY – BEYOND THE NUMBERS

When we teach any topics, we start with the fundamentals. For example, before we teach reading, we teach the A B C's. When we teach the A B C's, we teach the fundamental laws of pronunciation, such as how "A" is pronounced.

Before we teach Math, Trigonometry, or Calculus, we start with 1 2 3. We define 1 as not being 2 or 3 but a singular unit. We define 1 as a singular. It does not matter if we are using ordinal numbers or Roman Numerals; the concept or fundamental laws of the numbers are the same.

Instead of teaching the fundamentals of MONEY, we jump right into ECONOMICS, thinking that having learned reading, numbers, and some level of math is sufficient to understand economics. This ignores the teaching of the fundamental natural laws of money.

It does not teach that the dollar (or another monetary unit) has a defined worth but does not have a specified value. An item in a store may sell 9 for a dollar, and in another store, sell 10 for a dollar. So, this leaves the question, is the dollar value 9 or 10 items?

One farmer may wish to sell a bushel of wheat for a dollar, and another may want to sell a bushel of corn for a dollar. The first farmer may accept a dollar from the second farmer for his bushel of wheat but may not need a bushel of corn. The second farmer may sell the bushel of corn to someone else for a dollar. This illustrates a couple of things: One, in barter trade, the two farmers could have just exchanged the wheat for the corn without any money. This frequently proves inconvenient if one or the other does not need one of the items. Therefore, the use of money allows singular exchanges of items.

If the first farmer decides he wishes to sell his bushel of wheat for two dollars, the second farmer, wanting to make the trade, also decided that his bushel of corn should sell for two dollars. We now have dollar inflation, but the underlying value of a bushel of wheat and a bushel or corn has not changed as they will still produce the same number of loaves of bread or the same amount of cornmeal. So, while the "worth" of the items may have changed, the "underlying value" of the items has not. Basically, an increase in "worth" without an increase in value is "Inflation"!

Another fundamental of money is that you cannot spend the same dollar twice. Suppose you have 10 kids and give them each $100. After a while, they all pay you back that $100. Did you just make $1,000? No, you received worth of $1,000 without any increase in value. It is the same money you already had. Would you consider that taxable income? That may have seemed trivial, but the Government does this all the time, and it inflates their revenue so that they think they have more money to spend. This is also how many governments have collapsed under the eventual debt incurred.

Out of this illustration, a fundamental is born: No government spending produces real and usable tax dollars. The dollars collected in taxes from these expenditures is money that already belonged to the Government. Another fundamental that goes along with this is that the only REAL tax money comes from the private sector economy. Therefore, as the Government economy grows, and the Private sector economy shrinks, the amount of real tax revenue also shrinks!

It brings us to a fundamental or natural law of TAX. The only place taxes are resolved or collected is when an item is consumed. For example, when you buy and consume a hamburger, all the taxes are collected or resolved - all the taxes paid by farmers for land and profits and taxes on/in any other things he might have purchased during production. The same is true of the slaughter house, bakery, transportation, cooks, the establishment that made the final product.

All of these taxes, even though they may be individually minute, are in the price you paid for the hamburger. By the way, this may include sales tax, if applicable. If these were detailed, you would find that these are an appreciable part of the price. You no longer have the hamburger or the money you paid for it. The economy has now paid all of those taxes.

With all the taxes being paid at the time of "consumption," it leads us to another fundamental law of money. The rich are more tax collectors than taxpayers. They only pay real taxes on their consumption, and as the value of their consumption is usually greater than that of others, they do pay more taxes. But, the idea of taxing the rich more does not make sense. Take a high-income earner. If you take the time to look, you will see that income is generated by selling a product or service to many lower-income people. To stay in business, businesses must make more than their costs, so as taxes go up, so do their costs and the price they charge. Now, as we stated earlier, taxes are paid or resolved at consumption, the lower-income people are paying taxes when they consume these items. It makes the higher-income people more of tax collectors than taxpayers. Yes, they pay taxes on their income, but it ultimately comes from the lower-income consumers.

Therefore, raising taxes on the rich causes the lower-income classes to pay more taxes along with the strong possibility of forcing those people out of business. Another thing that needs to be understood is Bitcoin or Crypto Currency. It is my understanding that Casinos are required to keep as much cash on hand as they have in chip worth on the tables. It's done to ensure that there is a "value" behind those chips. Years ago, the dollar was pegged to a certain amount of gold or silver, giving tangible value to the money and ultimately to the chips. Now, there is no real asset linked to the dollar just as there is no tangible asset to the bitcoins or crypto currency. In other words, these worth's are free to be manipulated without any natural form of checks and balances.

I just remembered that back in the 50s or 60s, I seemed to come across a study that said that if the TOTAL TAX rate got above a certain point, the economy would become unsustainable or unbalanced. This would lead to runaway inflation. It seems to me that that number was somewhere in the mid-teen percentage. This would explain places like Venezuela, Zimbabwe, Greece, and many other countries that have lost control of their economy and have had runaway inflation.

I believe we are past that tipping point and are starting to feel the economy becoming out of control. I do not remember where or when I heard this number, and I do not know how to find it or the information it suggests.

THE DEATH OF BRICK AND MORTAR

Brick and mortar refer to the brick and mortar buildings that housed businesses for hundreds of years. These buildings and the businesses were the foundations of the communities, states, and, therefore, the country.

Many governments and politicians looked at these businesses as a source of revenue. These businesses had little major direct competition, so they were able to pass taxes on to the people who shopped there.

Being a largely rural country for many years, the politicians had to deal with their friends and neighbors. This meant that they would have to justify their need for taxes to people they would see every day. If they could not get their support, they could not pass the taxes they needed for their pet projects.

As the towns grew bigger, direct contact with all the people diminished. Thus, the politicians could pass taxes that many people, especially those in business, did not like. Back to the businesses, they had to pass these taxes on to the customers. The alternative was to go out of business and leave the community without their commodities or services. We need to look at how the finances of these businesses worked.

First, they needed to find a building that was fit for their needs and to house their business. This could be either a building that they rented or one that they bought. If it was a rental, they had to include the rent in their cost of doing business. If they bought a building, they probably had to borrow money to help buy it. Either way, the costs of having the building had to be covered by the profit that the business made. This is a cost that is added to the price that the proprietor paid for the item he is selling before he adds a profit to the item.

The "cost of doing business" is the sum of all expenses –things like rent, mortgage interest, proration of the cost of the building, or return on investment. Property tax is another item in the carrying cost that can make a big difference. Any interest on money borrowed to buy stock to sell, gas, electricity, to heat and light the business adds to the cost of doing business. Take a look at your electric, telephone, gas, and water bills. Look at the taxes that many of them itemize. Then there are the taxes paid by the owner and employees, which are not itemized but make a big difference in the carrying costs. These are a few of the fixed costs that must be recouped from the sale of goods or services.

Now, we look at indirect costs of doing business that the business owner has little, if any, control over. These include, but not limited to, taxes, insurance on the assets, liability insurance in case of injury, etc. They are a snapshot of the "fixed costs" of doing business. These costs must be covered every day regardless of the number of sales. If you sell more, the portion of the sales to cover these costs goes down. If you sell less, the portion goes up. These costs are sometimes called carrying costs. These are the costs that are added to an item daily. The longer an item sits on the shelf, the higher is its cost to the business and therefore requires a higher selling price.

This cost is a function of "inventory turns." Inventory turns are the frequency at which the value of your total inventory is replaced in a year. If the inventory turns once a year, the business needs to add enough to the selling price to cover the total fixed cost. If the inventory turns 2 times a year, half of that cost must be covered in each turn, etc.

Lastly, there are variable costs, such as the cost of help. If the business owner and their family run the business, they need to make enough profit to cover their taxes and cost of living. If one person can't handle the business, then family members might pitch in to help. This type of help can be added or reduced as the business demands change. For example, in a restaurant, you may need help only for the lunch rush for an hour, or two. This type of help's cost is already covered by the profits made. Therefore, it does not change the carrying cost of the business.

However, if you need to get outside help, there are more tax and legal restrictions that add to the variable costs of doing business. In cases where you only need an hour or two a day, you may need to carry more insurance and pay separate taxes for that person. If the need is for a full-time employee, you cannot easily make adjustments for seasonal or economic changes. This problem becomes easier the more employees you have.

Now, to the death of brick and mortar. People are blaming the big box stores and online retailers like Amazon. The big box stores mainly carry items that sell frequently. They, therefore, have higher inventory turns, meaning each item needs to cover less of the fixed and variable overhead costs. Also, they can flexibly schedule help to meet the demands, leading to a higher possibility of them selling at a lower price and still make the same or higher profit. Large online retailers have a bigger audience and therefore turn items faster. This means that they can carry items that move too slowly for brick and mortar or big box stores to handle. They then can cover broader customer needs in a single visit.

As we can see, fixed and variable costs, that we have discussed are significantly reduced for big box and online retailers. This also means that even though they may pay a higher dollar amount of taxes, the carrying costs per item become much higher for the brick and mortar business, thereby affecting profits of all types of businesses. The loss is higher for the low inventory turn businesses and much less for the high inventory businesses.

What I am saying is that taxing businesses has a more significant adverse effect on small businesses than on large businesses. This can drive the carrying costs of products up so high causing the smaller brick and mortar business to close.

Another problem then becomes the "efficiency experts" trying to find ways to cut costs. They will try to eliminate items that do not move rapidly to reduce the carrying costs. However, the downside to this is that it affects customers who come in for that item. This may cause them to look for another store or online. As my father told me many years ago, it is easier to lose a customer than to gain one. All this results in the elimination of brick and mortar businesses.

TAXATION – THE LAFFER CURVE AND GOVERNMENT DECEPTION

The Laffer curve is used to determine the maximum tax to charge to get the maximum return for the government. There are a lot of arguments about this curve and what it shows. My argument is that there are serious flaws in the accepted assumptions for the curve. If you look at the napkin that Art Laffer used to draw what has become known as the Laffer curve, you will see that he stated (without detail) some of the constraints that he placed on the curve. There are many subtleties involved in those constraints that are not readily obvious. In many of the subsequent attempted applications of his concept, some of his constraints and their subtleties are not implemented in their arguments.

As I said, they are trying to maximize revenue to the government. They include all tax revenue as if it is real. As I have shown in this book, taxes collected from government spending of that revenue are not real. The government hands an employee (for example) some money every week and then requires that person to pay $100 in tax. The person has to report the $100 as income, and the IRS reports the $100 as revenue. The man must pay tax on his portion as well as on what he keeps. After a year, the man has received and given back to the government $5200. All this time, it is just the same $100 that keeps going back and forth. This $5200 is not there and, therefore, not usable and should not be counted in the tax revenue or the economy.

This means that part of that Laffer curve is based on tax revenue that does not really exist because of subtleties that are part of what Mr. Laffer mentioned. Another part of the problem is that there is a minimum amount of money that people need to retain to be able to survive. This is not as obvious in the comments Mr. Laffer made, but it is an important part of the constraints, especially regarding the lowest income bracket. You may say that those people do not pay taxes. Taxes are settled when items are consumed, which is when a person buys a hamburger, he exchanges his money for that burger. In the price of that burger are all the taxes that were collected in producing it. As long as he has the burger, that money is still in its value. As soon as he consumes it, that value is gone! He has just paid all the taxes that were in the price. On top of that, he may have to pay an additional sales tax on things he consumes. So, the idea that the lower classes may not pay taxes is false.

As taxes are raised and incorporated into products or services, the price of these items goes up, and if it gets too high, it will drive people out of the economy. This too is not accounted for in the Laffer curve arguments. And, it is especially true of the lower-income class trying to live on minimum wage. As the tax rates and tax collections go up in the higher income brackets, the cost of essentials also goes up to cover these taxes. The effective income of those on minimum wage goes down. Not only is the amount of "payroll" tax paid by the employer reduces their actual buying power, but the embedded taxes in the products they buy also reduces their buying power. The thing that is not included in Laffer Curve calculations is the sharp drop that starts to occur when those on minimum wage can no longer make ends meet and drop out of the economy. Not only are they not contributing to the economy, but they are also becoming a drag on the tax-based assistance programs, which causes the need for more taxes.

The above is one of the main problems of those who think the Government can support helping all the people. The more support they try to give, the more people who can't make ends meet and require more assistance. This becomes a vicious circle. The problem of the tax rate is further confused by the fact that those using the curve are usually trying to justify tax rates for the federal government. They do not include the other taxes by states, counties, cities, local taxing agencies, etc.

The government is actually all of these. Federal Government could collect all of these taxes and distribute them to the individual entities, and the results would be the same. The only real way to maximize revenue is to minimize expenses. There are some fundamental things that the government should pay for, including military, courts, major roads, and the like. These are things that our Founding Fathers foresaw the government taking care of. They directly help the private sector that pays the tax. The government is now paying for things that do not directly benefit the person paying the tax. These things diminish the value of the hard-working minimum wage earners.

Remember, all taxes are paid by the end consumer. The lower-income classes spend their money on things that are immediately consumed. Therefore, they pay the most of their income on taxes. Politicians say they are going to raise taxes to help the lower-income people, but they are the ones that pay the most in taxes. As to the Laffer curve and the comments on the napkin, these items were just a quick high-level look at the problem with minimal constraints. I do not think that Mr. Laffer meant it to be an all-inclusive discussion as people are trying to make it out to be. I think it was just meant to be a 100,000-foot level quick view of the problem.

An innovative country needs rich people. Many innovations, especially in the healthcare field, take many millions of dollars to bring to market. Except for the very rich and their risk capital, there are not many ways to get these innovations to market. Are you going to bet everything you have and more on someone's idea that might or might not prove to be valuable? No, of course not. Rich people have money they can risk without jeopardizing their financial and family obligations. They have the capital to make large gambles or risky investments. Sometimes they are colossal failures, and they lose their capital. Quite frequently, they lose some or all of their investment, and other times they make a reasonable return. At other times, they may make a very sizeable return. It is these sizeable returns that make it possible for these people to gamble on innovation.

Right now, people are trying to get the government deeper into the healthcare industry. The problem with that is that many people that want to run things like this are very much risk avoidant! They will spend a fortune on reports and studies before they would consider investing in new products.

As an example, there is a company working on nuclear fusion. The government is doing some funding in this area. That company is getting its funding from private sector companies. When it finds it needs to change its approach, they make the change. Whereas if the government was involved, they would have to go before the government controllers and try to explain what they have found and why they need to scrap what they have and move in a different direction. For the most part, these government people do not fully understand what the people are talking about, and they would have to get many higher up committees to approve any new funding and/or change in direction.

The problem here is that trying to make the change in direction under government control could take years of wasted time while getting the private sector to approve the change, and the need for more risk capital may only need a discussion with one or two people. This could mean they could start immediately on making the change, which would probably mean that the change could be implemented. Discoveries could be made before the government bureaucracy could even make a decision.

The same applies to healthcare advances. It takes people with risk capital to fund the advancements. One of the problems is that many of the ideas do not pan out. Therefore, there is a loss of that risk capital. Some of the new attempts lead to different results than are expected. Even though these different results could find other uses that were not thought of, finally, the work could lead to something of great value. This advancement could have taken a long time to produce, and after that, it could take a long time and a lot of testing to get it approved by, say, the FDA. All of this time, lots of money is being spent keeping the project going (risk capital).

If the government is in control of the healthcare system, they may look at the advancement and decide it cannot be implemented because they already have something similar, even though it is not as effective, but it is much cheaper. With this hanging over innovation, not many companies will be willing to invest in innovation as a result, even if the idea is excellent, would be too much in doubt. Just briefly, another group of companies that people feel that are excessively rich is the Insurance industry. Yes, Insurance companies have quite a bit of money, and it is normally invested in many assets. The question becomes if all the policies they hold were to suffer the maximum expense suddenly, would the companies have enough assets to cover it? In other words, does the company have enough assets to cover its maximum liability? Probably not! They need to have enough assets and income to cover a reasonable amount of liability every year.

They also need enough assets to cover those times they have an unusual amount of liability to pay out. But even at that, I do not think any of the companies have the assets should they have to pay all their liabilities. So, while everyone thinks they are rich, they may be vulnerable to complete loss if something unusual should happen. They are not as rich as everyone thinks.

Another way to look at taxes is that the time that the money is "collected" from people and companies is when the Government is just borrowing from the product or service. This loan stays with the product or service. As this loan moves through the system, profits and other costs add to the amount of the loan, just like interest on your loans. When the product or service is consumed, the loan and all the accrued "interest" is paid off by the end-user. If this is an intermediate step, the loan is added to the next level of use.

If you have trouble following some of this, you might take a little advice, like I remember hearing Julie Andrews had given to her daughter when she was having trouble understanding something. She said she told her daughter to "stand on her head." I take this to mean she was telling her to turn the picture over and look at the problem. We tend to continue to look at the problem the same way we did when we first looked at it. Sometimes it helps to look at the problem from a different perspective! (Hopefully, that is what I am accomplishing here).

Misunderstood money and the political divide between rural and urban areas.

One of the things I have noticed about the politics of rural and urban areas is how these areas learn about the fundamentals of money. In rural areas, more people deal directly with the fundamentals of money daily. People who own small business, ranches, farms, etc. These people have to deal with the facts of life and the facts of money daily. They know that if they do not sell products and make a profit, they will not stay in business. Ranchers know that if they do not take care of their livestock, they will not have anything to sell. Farmers know that if they do not plant and harvest, they will not have any income.

Their families work together, seeing that things that need to be done are done. This results in everyone in the family getting some education on how money works. Even the hired help gets some insight into how money works in these businesses. Everyone sees that the owners that started these businesses probably had to borrow and hock everything, including their shorts, to start the business. They worked from sun-up to sundown and probably more, to make things work. These people probably did not eat more than beans for months and even years trying to pay back loans so that they can start making money from their investment.

Being in rural areas, people tended to see what others are doing and how they are struggling to make their businesses grow. From this proximity, they learned how money works. In urban areas, the majority of people work for someone else. They are distant from the people who started the businesses and did not see the risks and hardships the people went through to get these businesses to grow. Urban folks only think that working for someone else is going to work for some rich guy without any understanding of how the job was created or what the original owners went through to get to where they had a job to offer. They tend not to be "invested" in their job. They are not worried about the business as much as rural folks are. They have the opinion that if this job does not work out, they can go down the street and get another job. They tend to be less connected to the business and the people in it than are the rural workers.

Most of all, they are not interested in understanding how the money and finances of a business work as long as they get their paycheck. Along with this, they go to work and come home and do not discuss anything about how the business is doing or how the finances of the business are doing. This means the family and especially the children are not being given any exposure to how money actually works. They do not understand much more than see dollar, spend dollar.

So, while the people in the rural areas are, of necessity or through association with business owners, learning how money works, those in the urban areas are much more distant from the financial running of the business and do not get firsthand knowledge of how money works. I believe that this is why big businesses and corporations workers do not understand simple facts about money, such as that raising wages hurts them or that lower-income classes pay most of the taxes, and the rich are becoming more of just tax collectors.

TAX PAYERS AND TAX COLLECTORS

Everyone is a taxpayer that purchases anything from someone else's work and consumes it. The seller, to make any profit, must include any taxes he pays in the price he charges for his product. Therefore, a product or service must have the accumulation of all the taxes collected from all contributors. When the final purchaser consumes the product, the money he paid for that good or service is the ultimate source of the tax revenue.

Given this, and looking at the lower-income class, you can see that they will pay the most of their income to pay the accumulated taxes on the things they buy. These people need to spend most of their money on immediate consumables to live; they do not have much choice. This also means that any tax increases upstream have a more immediate and devastating effect on them.

For me, this is the reason all these politicians that talk about helping the poor by raising taxes elsewhere are actually increasing the tax burden on the lowest income classes the most. This is true even though this class may not pay any direct tax money other than sales tax and a few other possible taxes. One of which is the payroll tax. The people are led to believe that the employer is paying this tax. This tax would not be paid if there were no employees; therefore, it is part of the employee's pay. For those on minimum wage, they need to consider that their actual minimum wage pay is the minimum wage plus this payroll tax!

As for these direct taxes paid by these people, they are not the real people who pay these taxes. These taxes come out of their income, and their income comes from the people who buy the products and services they create. Again, it is those people who consume these products and services that actually settle or pay the tax.

I should probably give a better explanation of how the consumption of a good or service is the point at which taxes are paid on a product or service. Let's say you buy a hamburger for $5.00. That means that you had $5.00, and you exchanged it with someone else for the Hamburger. That means that you had $5.00, and he had a Hamburger worth $5.00. You make the exchange, and he now has the $5.00, and you have the Hamburger. The values are maintained in the transaction.

Now, you eat the Hamburger, meaning that you no longer have the worth of the hamburger, but he still has the $5.00. The $5.00 worth of the hamburger has been destroyed (by you). So, all of a sudden, the $5.00 for the hamburger no longer exists. Yes, the act of living destroys value, and unless some action to replace the value is taken, there will eventually be no value left to sustain life. Included in the $5.00 price of the hamburger is the tax paid by the vendor, and the suppliers of the meat and buns. The suppliers of the meat and buns get their raw materials from other suppliers who include their taxes in their price. These suppliers get their materials from the farmers and ranchers who pay taxes and also pay taxes on their land and earnings. All of these taxes and inflation along the way add profit markups of the various levels handling the product end up being paid by the end consumer.

This is where there becomes a problem with government spending. They keep supplying money to be "destroyed" without any action by the government to replace it other than to make other people supply the replacement. The government does not generate any "new" value. But I digress. As we move slowly up the economic ladder, we come to those that are just above the lowest economic class.

This class starts to see people who have small amounts of disposable income. It then gives them the opportunity to make choices with some of their income. They can choose to spend it on consumables or hold on to it for future use. If they choose to spend it, they again are immediately settling or paying all the taxes involved in the creation of the product or service.

If they choose to save it, they may be able to use it to generate extra income and gain a little advantage because this money has not yet been used to settle taxes. At some point, as we move up this economic ladder, people start to make enough money that they will be required to pay direct taxes to the Government. The thing of it is, they do not actually "pay" direct taxes. They only take the money they have collected from the products or services they provided and pass it on to the Government. The tax becomes part of the goods or services provided and sits there to be paid by the end consumer.

It is at this point in the economic ladder that people transition from full taxpayers to taxpayers and tax collectors. While in these lower economic classes, the amount of taxes these people pay (in their purchases) is higher than the taxes they collect through paying taxes on their earnings, they are moving toward becoming government tax collectors.

This group also starts paying more substantial taxes as the items they purchase are becoming more expensive, and the amount of taxes hidden in them becomes greater. At this point, we are starting to get into the income classes that are starting to have the ability to buy things like homes etc. The government likes to see this as there is a new source of revenue. Not only does the home price include the taxes collected by all the people involved in its manufacture, but it becomes an opportunity to tax "inflation."

This is inflation caused by arbitrary increases in wages. By this I mean raises in wages without any increase in value created by the job. Minimum wage raises and union across the board raises are a good example of inflationary raises. For example, in 2010 I had a property that was worth $165,000. In 2020 that same property had a valued worth of $289,626.

This is an increase in worth of 43.03%. If you divide the worth at each point by the minimum wage rate at that time and take the difference, you will see the "value" of the property only went up by 5.70%. While the value of the property did not really change, due to the location becoming more desirable, the property became slightly more valuable.

This means that if I sell the property at the current market worth, I would have to pay taxes on $124,626 in gains as opposed to taxes on the approximately $9,413 increase in value due to changes in value associated with the location. The extra taxes are taxes caused by this inflation, and the politicians love to have inflation for this very reason.

Back to the economic class ladder.

We are now getting to the level where more money than is needed is being saved to be spent on providing basic necessities. While these people are paying more and more taxes through their spending and purchases, they are now starting to save and invest. Some of these investments are paying immediate returns while others are deferring returns (such as homes) until later. If they generate new value, they will all be taxed at some point. What to remember here is that any taxes they generate comes from the source of value and are just being collected by the investor from the source of the investment. That is to say, owners of these investments are only tax collectors collecting money from the products produced by the investments. This is an iterative process down through all the levels of production until it is finally consumed, and the taxes are settled.

These investments must return a profit, or investors will not be interested in the investment and the probable jobs that it would create. It then means that even though the direct taxes on the invested value may be 10-20% or more, the investment must still return sufficient return to make it attractive to the investor. So, there must be enough to pay that 10-20% tax on the invested "company" there must be at least another 5-10% or more (depending on risk) for the investor to be interested. This would be after the direct taxes he must pay in that income.

By the way, it's also an example how taxes at various levels of a products development tend to get inflated throughout the process. Taxes, early in a production cycle, can become a more significant percentage of the final product price. Now, we get to the highest level of the economic ladder where people are only "spending" a small portion of their income, and they are investing a larger portion thereof. These investments are being taxed at the "manufacturing" level, and then after these direct taxes are paid, the profits are then taxed. After this, the investors get their return, which is then taxed again. But what is happening here?

1. Profits are being taxed multiple times, and

2. These taxes are ultimately being paid by the end-users, not the corporations or investors, and

3. These corporations and investors are collecting more taxes for the government than they are paying or "settling."

On the back of the above, the more you tax higher income levels than other levels, the more the taxes being paid or "settled" by the lowest income levels get raised indirectly and proportionally to the raises in tax rates for the upper levels. In other words, taxing the rich more heavily is actually taxing the lower classes as at this point, the rich are only tax collectors! While many people may disagree with this statement, I would suggest that they take the time and do the complete math on this and be careful what assumptions they make along the way.

We can use this to illustrate the problem that people on minimum wage are not ending up with enough to provide for themselves and their families. Between the hidden taxes, the payroll tax (which is part of their pay), the fact that no government spending produces "real" revenue, it is the private sector minimum wage earners that are carrying a hefty burden of the economy. The burden has gotten so heavy that many more people are ending up on the streets.

In my estimation, with roughly 7.5% that the "employer" pays, which is actually your pay, and the 7.5% that minimum wage earners pay along with the, 15-20% tax (in my estimation) hidden in the things they need to buy to survive, there is no way to live on that wage. And remember, the politicians are going to help you by raising more taxes to help. It is time for people to take notice that all the politicians who say they are going to help the lower economic class actually end up making it worse for them. Their ideas of taxing the rich actually take more money from the people they say they are going to help!

This discussion of how taxes eventually do not leave enough income for people to live is something I, for a long time, have been trying to quantify into the Laffer Curve model I have created. I have not been able to get numbers that are exact enough to generate an actual curve based on tax rates. These numbers reduce the actual value of the economy before you consider anything else. Therefore, the only thing I can do is give examples. At this point in time, homelessness and unemployment are growing, as are tax rates and debt. The politician's answer to these problems is for the government to spend more to put people on the government payroll. To the politicians, these people receiving an income will generate more tax revenue for the government to help cover the costs. This revenue is imaginary as this type of government spending cannot mathematically generate "real" taxes.

As the government tries to spend more of these imaginary taxes to help reduce the problem of homelessness and unemployment, the burden becomes heavier on the private sector real taxpayers. As this happens, the taxes that are included in the products and services they produce goes up. As these taxes go up, the cost of the goods goes up, and also the prices go up. As the prices go up, the ability of more people to afford the product goes down. With this increase in the prices, inflation, more people are pushed into homelessness and unemployment because they are not making enough to pay for the things they need. This rekindles the vicious circle of politicians trying to solve the problem by spending more government funds.

Let's look at an example from history. During the Great Depression, there were great numbers of homeless people trying to survive. The private sector economy was struggling to absorb this problem while the government was trying to borrow and spend more money to solve the problem. The private sector was trying to produce more real value and more revenue to the government while the government was trying to produce more imaginary revenue to solve the problem. Fortunately, the private sector finally won out and pulled the country out of the depression.

I heard that there were books written by those in government, and were involved with putting together government programs to try to solve the problem. I have also heard that at least one of these authors admitted that the programs they put together might have done more harm than good. These programs may have actually prolonged and deepened the depression. Again, while I may not be able to quantify the numbers to apply them to the Laffer Curve, I think it can be seen that this dis-enfranchisement of people from the economy will be a big negative to the actual economy and a great reduction to the "real" tax revenue.

Also, the effect will be magnified as the tax rates go up. Along with that, the negative impact on retirement monies increases as tax rates and inflation go up.

PRINTING MONEY

Printing money does not improve the economy at all. The value of the printed money (and coins) is loosely based on an expected support value. As more money is printed, the more that support value is divided among the pieces of paper. Back when the dollar was pegged to a given amount of gold, printing more money did not create value. The worth of gold (its value did not change) started going up accordingly. It meant that each dollar's value kept dropping. Finally, they decided to break the link from the dollar to the given amount of gold. It happened because the amount of gold promised for the dollar had value more than that which was specified in the dollar.

This phenomenon led to the politicians realizing that they could manipulate the value of the dollar. They discovered that the dollar was not tied to anything real, which gave them a large degree of power over the money. Nowadays, with Crypto Currency, Bitcoins, and dollars, all having a "floating value," it means that these "currencies" have no actual value. They only have some arbitrary value that is very fluid. With all this, the value of any of the currencies continues to go down and those holding reserves in "dollars" need to watch it as the actual value evaporates.

LETTERS TO THE EDITOR

To our Congressmen,

I see that the Congress has just taken a couple of trillion dollars out of the real economy to try to create an imaginary economy where the revenue is actually Imaginary!

How do I know these revenues are imaginary, I have looked! I have done the math that the natural laws say and yes, the revenue received will be imaginary.

This is nothing new, the government has been booking imaginary revenue for ever. The thing of it is, the government's economy was small compared to the current governmental economy. Therefore, the effect of this imaginary revenue was lost in the rounding.

Now that the governmental economy has gotten so big, this imaginary revenue has become a large part of the government's "revenue". No one seems to care as this imaginary revenue is not available, they just keep on spending real revenue to cover the problem.

Moves like this are going to create a depression that will make the "Great Depression" look like a cake walk.

Now I understand that you folks want to double down on this problem with an infrastructure bill that will add another two trillion dollars to the imaginary economy. You folks seem to think that the revenue from that will help the economy. It will only create more imaginary revenue that you folks will spend to create more imaginary economy.

Someone up there needs to "man-up" and take a hard look at this problem before we become another Zimbabwe, Venezuela or even Greece. They all try or tried to live on their imaginary revenue.

The Zimbabwe and Venezuela government printing presses can not keep up with the ever-increasing need for larger denomination bills to keep up with their inflation caused by their imaginary revenue.

PRINTING DOLLARS

The Government is running their printing presses to print more dollars. The problem is that the Government CAN NOT print or create value. The value of the dollars is based on the value of the economy. The only ones that can create value are those in the private sector.

It is like a pie, where the number of slices or the size of the slice is the value of that piece. The Government printing dollars is like slicing the pie in more pieces which means each piece of is smaller and less valuable.

Not only are they making more slices, at the same time the "pie" is getting smaller. So, they are making more slices in a smaller pie.

The problem then becomes to make value they are borrowing money. This borrowed money will have to be paid back. They will have to raise taxes.

People who actually physically pay taxes are only tax collectors. The tax money they pay comes from the products or services they provide. The only time taxes are really paid or settled is when those products or services are consumed.

As the lower economic classes need most of their money to buy things they consume, they are paying the larges burden of these taxes.

These taxes are going to raise the cost of these products or services so high that the lower income classes will eventually not be able to afford all the products they need to survive.

Yes, this will probably lead to a depression worse than the 1930's depression.

MINIMUM WAGE INCREASE

The politicians want to raise the minimum wage supposedly to help the lower income people. Raising the minimum wage without an increase in output only increases the cost of the items they produce which increases the amount they need to purchase the things they need to survive. It becomes like a dog chasing its tail, never ending.

Increasing the wages moves all incomes up therefore moving more money into higher income brackets. This means the government will collect more taxes and value from all the people. This will also move many of the lower income people to a level where they will not get the help they may now be receiving.

While people may think that this will help the people, it will actually destroy a lot of value that is in the economy.

For example, the Federal minimum wage is currently $7.25 and the want to raise it to $15.00. Let's look at what raising the wage does to the Social Security Trust Fund which is at 2.89 trillion dollars. Divide this by $7.25 gives this roughly 399 billion minimum wage hours in the trust fund. If we raise the wage to $15 and divide that into the trust fund, we will see that there only roughly 192 billion minimum wage hours left in the trust fund. This means we have lost roughly 207 billion minimum wage hours from the fund. This will destroy the value of 207 billion hours saved. This will require 207 billion times $15.00 or 3.105 trillion dollars to put the fund back to its 399 billion minimum wage hours. The government will have to tax everyone to recover that money and this will hit those getting a minimum wage rase the hardest.

This not only hits the Social Security Trust fund but everyone's savings account, annuity, bonds, state pension funds, other federal pension funds, etc. This will mean the destruction of many trillions in value!

Well, I should not say the destruction as many in the middle to upper income classes and properly invested will gain a significant amount from this. Just not the lower income people.

Just like printing money, this will decrease the VALUE of the dollar.

Folks, you need to start looking at the amount of VALUE instead of the number of pieces of paper (dollars).

School Funding

I see the Schools are having the same trouble with their money that the lower income classes are struggling with.

The problem is that the taxes, both direct and imbedded, are eating up the value needed to maintain the level of funding needed. As usual, everyone thinks that more taxes will help the problem. It will not, it will only eat up more of the value needed to make purchases.

These taxes become imbedded in the things that are needed inflating the costs and causing the funding to cover less.

This is somewhat the school's problem as they are not teaching "MONEY". People do not understand how money works or how taxes work. It does not matter where the taxes are applied, all taxes are settled when the goods or services are consumed.

As for public schools, these supposed taxes are only a refund and the money is circulating on the books as you can not tax, tax! It only reduces the value the schools have to spend and does not add to the governmental income.

FREE MONEY?

I see that the politicians are thinking that the Stimulus and CARES acts money is free money for them to spend. They think that they do not have to take money from the lower classes to fund their dreams.

The Government (and all levels are just departments of the same Government) does not have money of its own! All of their money comes from the people and only the private sector people at that.

Unfortunately, it is the lower income classes that pay the greatest percentage of their income as taxes. Oh yes, they may not pay taxes directly but the taxes they pay are embedded in the things they need to buy to survive. The more the Government spends, the more they have to collect from these embedded taxes raising the cost to these people.

Just because the money is coming from Washington does not mean it is not being collected from the local folk!

Any taxes collected from where ever, end up being embedded taxes in products being consumed. The upper classes do not need to spend all their money on consumption to survive so they do not get hit with the immediate taxes.

This embedded tax is not leaving enough "value" in the money the lower class needs to survive to purchase the things they need. This is why we are seeing more people living on the streets.

This is just like crossing the street, we need to look to the left and right as well as just looking straight ahead especially with a depression looming!

By the way, this free money idea applies to the credit cards. The stores raise the prices to cover the cost of the "free money" people are getting back. The little guy pays!

ECONOMIC STIMULUS

The government has spent all their rainy-day funds so they will have to borrow the money they are spending on economic stimulus. They will have to raise taxes to pay for their large stimulus spending. This will cause the prices of things to go up. This will mean that people will have less value in their income.

To cover the price increase wages will go up, thus causing prices to go up further. The consumer price index will go up meaning that those payments covered by C.O.L.A. will go up requiring taxes to go up to cover the larger payments.

With taxes and prices going up, minimum wages will have to be raised, again causing prices to go up. With minimum wages going up, retirement savings including Social Security trust fund will cover less payments. This again means that taxes will have to be raised to back fill those retirement funds. Personal savings will also lose value meaning people will have to try to back fill their savings.

All of this will start the cycle all over. With the massive amounts of spending going on and the massive debt incurred, I am not sure that the government will be able to collect enough taxes to cover the debt and other obligations. I fear that this will lead to a depression like the one in the 1920-1930's and possibly worse. In fact, the politicians are already making the same mistakes as were made back then. They need to go back and look at what happened then and what they learned.

This leads me to the question "aren't there any adults in the legislatures that understand how money naturally works?'

By the way, doesn't any one realize that taxes collected on government spending are just a rebate and not actually new money to the treasury?

www.ingramcontent.com/pod-product-compliance
Lightning Source LLC
LaVergne TN
LVHW041537060526
838200LV00037B/1030